AF651485

CONSTITUTIONAL SAFEGUARDS FOR WEAKER SECTIONS AND THE MINORITIES IN INDIA

About the Authors

Dr. Bindeshwar Pathak is a great humanist, social reformer, Founder of Sulabh Sanitation Movement and prolific writer. After Gandhi, Dr. Pathak is the man, more than any other in India, who has made upliftment of untouchables as mission of his life. For the last three decades, he has been working relentlessly to keep the ecosystem clean and bring the marginalised sections of society into the mainstream. He gave a new dimension to the Gandhian movement and broadbased his principled fight against all kinds of discriminations. Dr. Pathak has been advocating introduction of Action Sociology in the academic curriculum. Dr. Pathak has authored several well-received books including *Road to Freedom, Man and His Mission, Social Justice and Development of Weaker Sections, Sulabh Śhauchalaya: A Study of Directed Change, Sulabh Shauchalaya: A Simple Idea that Worked, Action Sociology and Development, Rural Violence in Bihar, Mukti ke Marg Par.* Besides Padma Bhushan, Dr. Pathak is also recipient of several national and international awards including the prestigious St. Francis Prize for the Environment, Italy.

Mr. B.N. Srivastava is a social activist, planner and administrator who served the Government of India and held several prestigious positions, including in the Ministry of Home Affairs, Ministry of Welfare, etc. As a planner, he formulated strategies for rapid development of weaker sections. He made valuable contributions in the implementation of several developmental programmes meant for weaker sections. At present, Shri Srivastava is Hony. Chairman (Administration), in the Sulabh International Social Service Organisation.

A prolific writer Shri Srivastava has to his credit books and research articles published in journals in India and abroad. The *Statesman* described his latest book *Manual Scavenging in India – A Disgrace to the Country* as a scholarly work and a unique treatise, a goldmine for researchers.

CONSTITUTIONAL SAFEGUARDS FOR WEAKER SECTIONS AND THE MINORITIES IN INDIA

BINDESHWAR PATHAK

B.N. SRIVASTAVA

CONCEPT PUBLISHING COMPANY, NEW DELHI-110059

All rights reserved. No part of this work may be reproduced, stored in a retrieval system, or transmitted in any form or by any means, electronic, mechanical, photocopying, recording or otherwise, without the prior written permission of the copyright owner and the publisher.

ISBN. 81-7022-746-1

First Published 1999

© Authors

Published and Printed by
Ashok Kumar Mittal
Concept Publishing Company
A/15-16, Commercial Block, Mohan Garden
New Delhi-110059 (India)

Phones : 5648039, 5649024
Fax : 091-11-5648053

PREFACE

Forty and eight years ago was founded the sovereign socialist secular democratic Republic of India with the fourfold objective of securing to its citizens justice, liberty, equality and fraternity. Eminent persons of the highest order – the like of which this country has not seen since – belonging to the different fields such as law, politics and public life came together to frame the Constitution of India. Our Constitution like many modern constitutions was also, *'a break with the past'* and was framed with *'a need for fresh look'*. Centuries of deliberate and concerted effort to deface the society by creating caste consciousness and exploiting religious sentiments was effaced by the learned framers of the Constitution. In every free country which has adopted a system of governance through democratic principles, the people have their fundamental inalienable rights and enjoy the recognition of inherent dignity and of equality analogous to the rights proclaimed in the 'Bill of Rights' in USA, the 'Rights of Man' in the French Constitution of 1971 and Universal Declaration of Human Rights, 1948. The Indian Constitution is unquestionably unique in its character and assimilation having its notable aspirations contained in Fundamental Rights through which the illumination of Constitutional rights comes to us with the motto of equal distribution of justice in the social, political and economic spheres. The 'Fundamental Rights' and Part-IV of Indian Constitution dealing with 'Directive Principles of State Policy' which represent the core of the Indian Constitutional philosophy envisage the methodology for removal of historic injustice and inequalities – either inherited or artificially created – and social and economic disparity and ultimately for achieving an egalitarian society in terms of the basic structure of our Constitution as spelt out by the preamble.

Economic backwardness is the bane of the majority of the people in the country. There are poor sections in all the castes and communities which vary from section to section of the people. While the social and educational backwardness may be more pronounce in the case of the so-called lower castes or occupational groups, the economic backwardness is common to all irrespective of caste, creed or religion. Article 46 enjoins upon the State to promote with special care the educational and economic interests of the "weaker sections" of the people, and, in particular, of the Scheduled Castes and Scheduled Tribes and to protect, them from social injustice and all forms of exploitation. "The expression 'weaker section' of the people is obviously wider than the expression "backward class" of citizens in Article 16(4) which is only a part of the weaker section as whole while the same words occurring in Article 15(4) are followed by a qualifying phrase "socially and educationally". In the course of debate in the Parliament on Article 10(1) and 10(3) of the Draft Constitution which corresponded to Article 16(1) and 16(4) of the Constitution, Dr. B.R. Ambedkar, the then Minister for Law and Chairman of the Draft Committee expressed his views that "backward classes are nothing else but collection of certain castes."

The Constitution of India provides for a number of safeguards for the Scheduled Castes, Scheduled Tribes, Backward Classes and the Minorities which are one of its unique features. The safeguards have apparently helped these communities in protecting their legitimate interests and accelerated their socio-economic development. The credit for incorporating these safeguards in the Constitution of India goes to Dr. Bhimrao Ramji Ambedkar, Chairman of the Drafting Committee of the Constitution. It is but for him our Constitution would not have had this distinctive dimension.

After the announcement of the so-called Communal Award on 17 August, 1932 by the then British Prime Minister, Ramsay MacDonald under which the depressed classes were for the first time recognised as minority community and were granted assured representation with separate electorate for a period of twenty years, Mahatma Gandhi resolved to fast unto death unless that part of the

Award was rescinded as according to him it was a severe blow to the unity of the Independence movement. The British were unwilling to climb down and Gandhi's fast began as scheduled. It was Dr. Ambedkar who had pressed for a separate minority status for the depressed classes at the Round Table Conference in London the previous year. Dr. Ambedkar's immediate concern was to save Gandhi's life as well as national unity. He insisted, however, that each side had to give before an agreement could be reached. Gandhiji was opposed to separate electorate but was agreeable to reservation of seats. Dr. Ambedkar asked for large increase in the number of seats as a price for accepting joint electorates. In the end, both sides agreed to the principle of proportional representation which could give the depressed classes 147 seats; more than twice as many as originally granted. In addition to the 147 seats in the Provincial Legislatures, 18 per cent of the general electorate seats in the Central Legislature were to be reserved for these classes. This agreement, known as the Poona Pact was reached on 24 September 1932. The crisis was over and Gandhiji broke his fast. It was thus under the able stewardship of Dr. Ambedkar the various safeguards to protect the interests of the weaker sections, particularly the Scheduled Castes, Scheduled Tribes, Backward Classes and the Minorities were incorporated in the Constitution of India.

In this small book, an attempt has been made to present all the safeguards provided in the Constitution of India for the Scheduled Castes, Scheduled Tribes, Backward Classes and the Minorities at one place. An attempt has also been made to give a brief running commentary on the working of some of them since the Constitution came into force. The purpose is to serve as a reference book but in case of doubt or for elaboration of any matter, reference should be had to the original source.

October, 1998 BINDESHWAR PATHAK

New Delhi B.N. SRIVASTAVA

INTRODUCTION

The Constitution of India came into effect on 26th January, 1950. The draft Constitution was drawn up by a Drafting Committee headed by Dr. B.R. Ambedkar published in February, 1948. It was finally adopted by the Constituent Assembly on November 26, 1949.

The Constituent Assembly was initially summoned for undivided India on December 9, 1946. With the partition of India finally decided in June, 1947, the members of the Constituent Assembly belonging to the areas now in Pakistan ceased to be members of the Assembly. On August 14, 1947, the Constituent Assembly met again as the Sovereign Constituent Assembly for the Dominion of India under the Presidentship of Sachchidananda Sinha. On the demise of Sinha, Dr. Rajendra Prasad became the President of the Assembly.

The Constitution of India closely follows the British Parliamentary model but differs from it in one important aspect that is, the Constitution is supreme, not the Parliament. The Indian Judiciary is, therefore, vested with the authority to adjudicate on the Constitutionality of any law passed by the Parliament.

The Indian Constitution consists of the following:

1. The Preamble
2. Parts I to XXII covering Articles 1 to 395
3. Schedules 1 to 12, and
4. An Appendix Part IX — The Panchayats and Schedule XI (Article 243-G) have been newly incorporated under 73rd Constitution Amendment Act, 1992.

PART – I

The Union and its Territory

1. Name and territory of the Union (a) India, that is Bharat, shall be a Union of States; (b) The States and Territories thereof shall be specified in the first Schedule; (c) the territories of the States; the Union Territories, such other territories as may be acquired; (2) Admission or establishment of new States; (3) Formation of new States and alteration of areas, boundaries or names of existing States.

Distribution of Power

The Union has exclusive power to make laws on all matters in List I of the Seventh Schedule (Union List). The States have exclusive power to make laws on all matters in List II (State List). The Union and States have concurrent powers to legislate on any matter enumerated in List III (Concurrent List).

Residuary Powers

The Union has exclusive power to make laws on any matter not enumerated in the Concurrent List or State List.

Over-riding Powers

In case of any conflict between Union laws and State laws, the Union laws shall prevail.

PART – II

Citizenship

Citizenship rights are given to every person who is born in India or who has been a resident of India for 5 years immediately preceding the commencement of the Constitution.

PART – III

Fundamental Rights

Fundamental Rights are granted to citizens under Article 12 to 35 – (a) Right to Equality; (b) Right to Freedom; (c) Right Against Exploitation; (d) Right to Freedom of Religion; (e) Cultural and Educational Rights; (f) Right to Constitutional Remedies.

PART – IV

Directive Principles of State Policy

The Directive Principles of State Policy are contained in Articles 36 to 51 of the Constitution with 19 objectives. The Directive Principles of State Policy enjoining the State to undertake within its means, a number of welfare measures. These are intended to assure citizens an adequate means of livelihood, raise the standard of living, improving public health, provide free and compulsory education for children and assure that the operation of the economic system does not result in the concentration of wealth and means of production to the detriment of the common good. These are not enforceable at law like Fundamental Rights. Nevertheless, they are declared fundamental to the governance of the country.

PART – IV - A

Fundamental Duties

The 42nd Amendment Act, 1976 was incorporated into the constitution a new Chapter on Fundamental Duties in Part IV-A and Article 51-A.

The Duties for an Indian citizen enshrined, include:

(a) to abide by the Constitution and respect its ideals and institutions, the National Flag and the National Anthem;

(b) to cherish and follow the noble ideals which inspired our freedom struggle;

(c) to uphold and protect the sovereignty, unity and integrity of India;

(d) to defend the country and render national service when called for;

(e) To promote harmony and the spirit of common brotherhood amongst all Indians and renounce practices derogatory to the dignity of women;

(f) to preserve the rich heritage of our composite culture;

(g) to protect and improve the natural environment including forests, lakes, rivers and wild life and to have compassion for living creatures;

(h) to develop the scientific temper, humanism and the spirit of enquiry and reform;

(i) to safeguard public property and to abjure violence;

(j) to strive towards excellence in all spheres of individual and collective activity so that the nation constantly rises to higher levels of endeavour and achievement.

Part – V : The Union

Chapter I – The Executive

The Executive: There shall be a President of India who is the Executive Head of State and the Supreme Commander of the Armed Forces.

The President shall be elected from an electoral college consisting of (a) the elected members of both Houses of Parliament and (b) the elected members of the Legislative Assemblies of the States. The President shall hold office for five years and is eligible for re-election.

The Vice-President shall be elected by the members of an electoral college consisting of the members of both Houses of Parliament. The Vice President may hold office for five years and shall be the ex-officio Chairman of the Council of States.

There shall be a Council of Ministers with the Prime Minister at the head to aid and advise the President in the exercise of his functions. The Prime Minister shall be appointed by the President, and the other Ministers shall be appointed by the President on the advice of the Prime Minister. The Ministers shall hold office during the pleasure of the President.

Chapter II

There shall be a Parliament for the Union, which shall consist of the President and two Houses, the Council of States (Rajya Sabha) and the House of the People (Lok Sabha).

In the Presidential system of government like that of the U.S.A., the three branches of government – the Legislature, the Executive and the judiciary – are independent units. But in a Parliamentary system like that of India, the Executive is subordinate to the Legislature. The judiciary alone functions as an independent unit.

Chapter III deals with the legislative powers of the President. Chapter IV, Part IV of the Constitution deals with judiciary. There shall be a Supreme Court of India, consisting of a Chief Justice of India and other judges. The Parliament has the power to increase the number of judges.

A judge of the Supreme Court is to be appointed by the President after consultation with the Chief Justice of the Supreme Court and shall hold office until the age of sixty-five and can be removed from office by the President, only after an address by each House of Parliament supported by more than two-thirds majority of members present and voting.

Chapter V – There shall be a Comptroller and Auditor General of India to be appointed by the President and an Election Commission.

Part – VI – The States

The Governor of a State is the Executive head of the State Government. He is assisted by a Council of Ministers, with the Chief Minister at the head. The Chief Minister is to be appointed by the Governor and other Ministers are to be appointed on the advice of the Chief Minister.

The Legislature of a State shall consist of the Governor and one or two Houses of legislature as the case may be. The Legislative Assembly of a State may consist of not more than 500 and not less than 60 members. The Union Territories ordinarily have no Council of Ministers or legislature of their own. But the Parliament may by law create for any of the Union Territories a body, whether elected or partly elected and partly nominated to function as a legislature for the Union Territory or a Council of Ministers or both.

Article 343 of the Constitution provides that the Official language of the Union shall be Hindi in the Devanagari script. English which was originally to continue as the Official language only upto January 25, 1965 will under the Official Languages Act, 1963 continue to be used in addition to Hindi.

Article 368 deals with Amendment of the Constitution. A Bill for Amendment must be passed in each House by a majority of the total membership of that House and by a majority of not less than two-thirds of the members present and voting.

Amendments to certain parts of the Constitution, however, require ratification of the Legislatures of not less than one-half of the States by resolutions to that effect.

There are Twelve Schedules to the Constitution. The Ninth Schedule was added by the First Amendment to the Constitution in 1951 and the 11th and 12th by the 73rd and 74th Amendments in 1992.

The Constitution of India contains several provisions to protect the interest of Weaker Sections and Minorities from exploitation and discrimination on the one hand, and provides for special privileges for their speedy development to equality with the rest of the population on the other until such time when their glaring deficiencies are removed. These special provisions have been discussed in detail in the subsequent Chapters.

CONTENTS

1

Articles of the Constitution of India Relevant to the Weaker Sections and the Minorities

Preamble

WE, THE PEOPLE OF INDIA, having solemnly resolved to constitute India into a SOVEREIGN SOCIALIST SECULAR DEMOCRATIC REPUBLIC and to secure to all its citizens:

JUSTICE, social, economic and political;

LIBERTY of thought, expression, belief, faith and worship;

EQUALITY of status and of opportunity; and to promote among them all;

FRATERNITY assuring the dignity of the individual and the unity and integrity of the Nation;

IN OUR CONSTITUENT ASSEMBLY this twenty-sixth day of November, 1949, do HEREBY ADOPT, ENACT AND GIVE TO OURSELVES THIS CONSTITUTION.

PART – III
FUNDAMENTAL RIGHTS

General

12. Definition – In this Part, unless the context otherwise requires, "the State" includes the Government and Parliament of

---

The Preamble contains the ideals and aspirations or the objects which the Constitution-makers intended to be realised, by its enacting provisions. Inserted by the Constitution (Twenty-fourth Amendment) Act, 1971.

India and the Government and the Legislature of each of the States and all local or other authorities within the territory of India or under the control of the Government of India.

13. Laws inconsistent with or in derogation of the fundamental rights – (1) All laws in force in the territory of India immediately before the commencement of this Constitution, in so far as they are inconsistent with the provisions of this Part, shall, to the extent of such inconsistency, be void.

(2) The State shall not make any law which takes away or abridges the rights conferred by this Part and any law made in contravention of this clause shall, to the extent of the contravention, be void.

(3) In this article, unless the context otherwise requires, —

(a) "law" includes any Ordinance, order, bye-law, rule, regulation, notification, custom or usage having in the territory of India the force of law;

(b) "laws in force" includes laws passed or made by a legislature or other competent authority in the territory of India before the commencement of this Constitution and not previously repealed, notwithstanding that any such law or any part thereof may not be then in operation either at all or in particular areas.

*[(4) Nothing in this article shall apply to any amendment of this Constitution made under article 368.]

RIGHT TO EQUALITY

Equality before Law

14. The State shall not deny to any person equality before the law or the equal protection of the laws within the territory of India.

---

* Inserted by the Constitution (Twenty-fourth Amendment) Act, 1971.

Prohibition of discrimination on Grounds of Religion, Race, Caste, Sex or Place of Birth

15(1) The State shall not discriminate any citizen on grounds only of religion, race, caste, sex, place of birth or any of them.

(2) No citizen shall, on grounds of religion, race, caste, sex, place of birth or any of them, be subjected to any disability, liability, restriction or condition with regard to–

(a) access to shops, public restaurants, hotels and places of public entertainment; or

(b) the use of wells, tanks, bathing ghats, roads and places of public resort maintained wholly or partly out of State, funds or dedicated to the use of the general public.

(3) Nothing in this article shall prevent the State from making any special provision for women and children.

(4)[1]Nothing in this article or in clause (2) of article 29 shall prevent the State from making any special[2] provision for the advancement of any socially and educationally backward classes of citizens or for the Scheduled Castes and the Scheduled Tribes.

Equality of Opportunity in Matters of Public Employment

16(1) There shall be equality of opportunity for all citizens in matters relating to employment or appointment to any office under the State.

---

1 Added by the Constitution (First Amendment) Act, 1951, s. 2.

2 There is a reservation of 15% for Scheduled Castes and 7.5% for Scheduled Tribes in the matter of admission in all the educational institutions which come under the administrative control of the Ministry of Human Resource Development and other Central Ministries. Similar reservations have also been provided by the State Governments and U.T. Administration.

(*Contd.*)

(2) No citizen shall, on grounds only of religion, race, caste, sex, descent, place of birth, residence or any of them, be ineligible for, or discriminated against in respect of, any employment or office under the State.

Educational facilities like scholarships/stipends, books and stationery, uniforms, mid-day meals, hostels, special coaching etc. are also provided to the students from these communities. There is no doubt that there has been considerable progress in the field of education. The literacy rate amongst the Scheduled Castes and Scheduled Tribes rose from 1.9% and 0.7% in 1931 to 37.41% and 29.60% respectively in 1991. Also, while in 1944-45, only 114 students belonging to Scheduled Castes and 84 Scheduled Tribes in 1948-49 received post-matric scholarships, this number rose to 22 lakh students in 1997-98.

(Source: Annual Report of Ministry of Social Justice and Empowerment for 1997-98.)

The Tamil Nadu Backward Classes, Scheduled Castes and Scheduled Tribes (reservation of seats in educational institutions and appointments or posts in the services under the State) Act, 1993. (The Tamil Nadu Act of 1994) providing for reservation to the extent of 60% has been enacted and included in the Ninth Schedule of the Constitution on 31st August 1994 as the Constitutional (76th Amendment) Bill, 1994. A writ petition was filed in the Supreme Court challenging the validity of the Tamil Nadu Act, the Supreme Court has referred the matter to the Constitution Bench. However, the operation of the Act has been stayed.

The Karnataka Scheduled Castes, Scheduled Tribes and Other Backward Classes (reservation of seats in educational institutions and appointment of posts in the services under the State) Bill, 1994 providing for reservation upto 73% was accorded President's assent on 23rd Oct. 1994. However, a writ petition was filed challenging the validity of this law. The Supreme Court in an interim order passed on 11th Nov. 1994 has restricted the total percentage of reservation to 50% only. The State Government has abided by this order. The Scheduled Castes constitute 16.48% and Scheduled Tribes 8.08% of the total population of the country (1991 Census).

National Backward Classes Finance and Development Corporation

National Backward Classes Finance and Development Corporation (NBCFDC) was set up by the Government of India under Ministry of Welfare on 13th January, 1992 as a company not for profit under Section 25 of the Companies Act with the objective of providing concessional finance to the

(Contd.)

(3)[3]Nothing in this article shall prevent Parliament from making any law prescribing, in regard to a class or classes of employment or appointment to an office [4](under the Government of, or any local or other authority within, a State or Union Territory, any requirement as to residence within that State or Union Territory) prior to such employment or appointment.

(4)[5]Nothing in this article shall prevent the State from making any provision for the reservation of appointments or posts in favour of any backward class of citizens which, in the opinion of the State, is not adequately represented in the services under the State.

(4A)[6]Nothing in this article shall prevent the State from making any provision for reservation in matters of promotions to any class or classes of posts in the services under the State in favour of the Scheduled Castes and the Scheduled Tribes which, in the opinion of the State, are not adequately represented in the services under the State.

---

members of backward classes living below double poverty line for their socio-economic development by extending them loans for income generating schemes. The Corporation undertakes: (a) to provide an additional channel of finance to backward classes for economically and financially viable schemes and projects and, (b) Upgrade the technological and entrepreneurial skills of individuals or groups belonging to Backward Classes. The authorised share capital of the Corporation was Rs. 200 crores which has now been raised to Rs. 700 crores. The paid up capital of the Corporation was 198.90 crores, as on 31st March, 1998. The Corporation has so far sanctioned loans amounting to Rs. 539.46 crores of which Rs. 268.74 crores were disbursed as on 31st March, 1998.

3. In Column (3) of Article 16, the reference to the State shall be construed as not including a reference to the State of Jammu & Kashmir.

4. Subs. by the Constitution (Seventy Amendment) Act, 1956, s. 29 and Schedule, for "under any State specified in the First Schedule or any local or other authority within its territory, any requirement as to residence within that State".

(5) Nothing in this article shall effect the operation of any law which provides that the incumbent of an office in connection

---

5. There is a reservation of 15% for Scheduled Castes, 7.5% for Scheduled Tribes and 27% for Other Backward classes in all the posts under the control of Central Government and Central Public Undertakings. Similar reservations have also been provided in the posts and services under the State Governments/UT Administrations. The percentage of such reservations which has been kept in proportion to the population of these communities, varies from State to State. Reservations have also been provided in posts filled by promotion. The reservation of more than 50 per cent of the vacancies as, they arise in any year or a 'carry forward' rule which has the same effect will be outside the provision of Art. 16(4). As a result of the implementation of the reservation policy, there has been a considerable increase in the representation of Scheduled Castes and Scheduled Tribes in various posts and services under the Central Government. In so far as the Scheduled Castes are concerned, their percentage of representation rose from 0.71, 2.01, 7.03 and 17.19 in Group A, B, C and D* respectively in 1957 to 10.15, 12.67, 16.15 and 21.26 respectively in 1995. The representation of Scheduled Tribes also rose from 0.10, 0.32, 0.62 and 2.44 in Group A, B, C and D* respectively in 1957 to 2.89, 2.68, 5.69 and 6.48 respectively in 1995. In the IAS the percentage of Scheduled Castes and Scheduled Tribes increased from 1.63 and 0.09 respectively in 1954 to 15.8 and 7.9 respectively in 1995. Similarly in IPS, this percentage for Scheduled Castes and Scheduled Tribes rose from 1.19 and 0.51 in 1954 to 15.6 and 8.3 in 1995. Insofar as other backward classes are concerned, the Govt. of India for the first time issued an Office Memorandum on the 13th August, 1990 providing reservation of 27% of the vacancies in civil posts and services under the Central Govt. for socially and educationally backward classes. The said order was to take place from 7.8.90. Writ petitions were filed in the Supreme Court questioning the said Memorandum alongwith the applications for staying the operation of the Memorandum. It was stayed by the Supreme Court. Another Office Memorandum was issued on 25th September, 1991 modifying the earlier Memorandum dated 13th August, 1990. The modified order provided that within the 27% of the vacancies in civil posts and services under the Govt. of India reserved for SEBC preference shall be given to candidates

(*Contd.*)

---

* Excluding sweepers (*Source*: Annual Report (1997-98) of the Ministry of Personnel, Public Grievances & Pensions).

with the affairs of any religious of denominational institution or any member of the governing body thereof shall be a person professing a particular religion or belonging to a particular denomination.

Abolition of Untouchability

17.[7] "Untouchability" is abolished and its practice in any form is forbidden. The enforcement of any disability arising out of

---

belonging to the poorer sections of the SEBCs. In case sufficient number of such candidates are not available, unfilled vacancies shall be filled by the other SEBC candidates. The above order also provided that 10% of the vacancies in civil posts and services under the Govt. of India shall be reserved for other economically backward sections of the people who are not covered by any of the existing schemes of reservation.

The Supreme Court in the judgement dated 16.11.92 in writ petition (civil) No. 930 of 1990, **Indra Sawhney etc. etc. vs. Union of India and others, etc. etc.** declared the OM dated 13.8.90 and 25.9.91 issued by the Government of India unenforceable for want of valid identification of backward classes of citizens qualified for reservation under Article 16 of the Constitution of India. The Apex Court directed the Govt. of India to re-examine the question of identification of the backward classes of citizens in accordance with the principles and directives contained in the respective judgements of 9 judge Constitution Bench of the Supreme Court in this case and pass appropriate orders providing for reservation under Article 16(4).

The Govt. of India appointed an Expert Committee to recommend the criteria for exclusion of the creamy layer, i.e. the socially advanced persons/sections from the benefits of reservation for Other Backward Classes in civil posts and services under the Govt. of India. Consequent to the consideration of the Expert Committee's recommendations, the Govt. have issued orders in modification of the orders, dated 13.8.90.

6. Clause (4A) inserted by the Constitution (77th Amendment) Act, 1995 with effect from 17.6.95.

7. The law to punish such offences took five years to arrive. The Untouchability (Offences) Act, 1955 came into force on 1.6.1955 and after a lapse of 17 years it was amended and renamed as the Protection of Civil Rights Act, 1955 in 1976 by making the punishments under this Act more stringent and offences non-compoundable. The machinery for the enforcement of this Act has been suitably strengthened by the setting up of special cells, special courts, mobile squads, provision of legal aid etc.

(*Contd.*)

'Untouchability' shall be an offence punishable in accordance with law.

RIGHT TO FREEDOM

19.[8] Protection of certain rights regarding freedom of speech etc.: (1) All citizens shall have the right,–

(a) to freedom of speech and expression;
(b) to assemble peacefully and without arms;
(c) to form associations or unions;
(d) to move freely throughout the territory of India;
(e) to reside and settle in any part of the territory of India; and[9]
(f) *******
(g) to practise any profession, or to carry on any occupation, trade or business.

One of the innovations of the Act is that every year the Central Government will place on the table of each house of the Parliament, a report on the measures taken by itself and by the State Governments in pursuance of the mandate contained in Sec. 15. Such reports have been laid on the table of both the houses. Though the prevalence of untouchability is on the decline, yet its prevalence is still reported, in one form or the other in some parts of the country. Over the years, the cases registered under the Act have been declining as will be seen from the following table:

1992	.....	3148
1993	.....	2681
1994	.....	1794
1995	.....	1599
1996	.....	1489
1997	.....	1304

One of the important requirements for the effective enforcement of any penal law is that the crime should normally be accompanied by punishment. Crime divorced from punishment is an invitation to licence the offenders. If the percentage of convictions and acquittals to total cases disposed of by the courts and the ratio of convictions to acquittals in the country is analysed, it will be seen that not only has the proportion of convictions never exceeded half of the acquittals, but compared to the earlier years, the proportion of convictions has flagged and fallen in

(*Contd.*)

(2)[9] Nothing in sub-clause (a) of (1) shall effect the operation of any existing law or prevent the State from making any law, in so far as such law imposes reasonable restrictions on the exercise of the right conferred by the said sub-clause in the interests of the sovereignty and integrity of India, the security of the State, friendly relations with foreign States, public order, decency or morality, or in relation to contempt of court, defamation or incitement to an offence.

(3) Nothing in sub-clause (b) of the said clause shall affect the operation of any existing law in so far as it imposes, or prevent the State from making any law imposing, in the interest of [10](the sovereignty and integrity of India or) public

---

subsequent years. The results achieved in some states show that other states could have done better in the matter of convictions and improved the all-India performance. The enforcement of the PCR Act in terms of cases registered, disposed of at different stages and levels from the police to the court and convictions, is not adequate. Very few states have taken seriously the establishment of Special Courts as per clause (iii) of sec 15A(2), preferably Mobile special courts. Delay for want of quick trials through exclusive special and mobile courts results in the State, unintentionally though but not unwittingly, promoting acquittals, leaving enough time for complainants and witnesses to be reduced to silence. (*Source*: Annual Report of the Ministry of Social Justice and Empowerment for 1997-98)

8. In its application to the State of Jammu & Kashmir, for a period of twenty five years from the 14th May, 1954, act 19 shall be subject to the following modifications:-
   (i) In clauses (3) and (4), after the words "in the interests of", the words "the security of the State or" shall be inserted;
   (ii) In clause (5), for the words "or for the protection of interest of any Scheduled Tribe", the world "or in the interest of the security of the State" shall be substituted; and
   (iii) the following new clause shall be added, namely: (7) The words "reasonable restriction" occurring in clauses (2), (3), (4) and (5) shall be construed as meaning such restrictions as the appropriate Legislature deems reasonable."

9. Subs. by the Constitution (First Amendment) Act, 1951, s.3, for the original Cl. (2) with (retrospective effect).

10. "And" inserted and sub-Cl. (f) omitted by the Constitution by (44th Amendment) Act, 1978 w.e.f. 20.6.1979).

order, reasonable restrictions on the exercise of the right conferred by the said sub-clause.

(4) Nothing in sub-clause (c) of the said clause shall affect the operation of any existing law in so far as it imposes, or prevent the State from making any law imposing, in the interests of [11](the sovereignty and integrity of India or) public order or morality, reasonable restrictions on the exercise of the right conferred by the said sub-clause.

(5) Nothing in sub-clauses (d), and (e) of the said clause shall affect the operation of any existing law in so far as it imposes, or prevent the State from making any law imposing, reasonable restrictions on the exercise of any of the rights conferred by the said sub-clauses either in the interests of the general public or for the protection of the interests of any Scheduled Tribe.

(6) Nothing in sub-clause (g) of the said clause shall affect the operation of any existing law in so far as it imposes, or prevent the State from making any law imposing, in the interests of the general public, reasonable restrictions on the exercise of the right conferred by the said sub-clause, and, in particular [12](nothing in the said sub-clause shall affect the operation of any existing law in so far as it relates to, or prevent the State from making any law relating to:

(i) the professional or technical qualifications necessary for practising any profession or carrying on any occupation, trade or business, or

---

11. Ins. by the Constitution (Sixteenth Amendment) Act, 1963, s. 2
12. Subs. by the Constitution (First Amendment) Act, 1951, s. for certain original words. 2-225 M. of H.A./78.
13. The Bonded Labour System (Abolition) Act, 1976 was enacted with a view to abolishing this evil practice and making the offences under this Act punishable. Under a Centrally Sponsored Programme grant-in-aid is provided to the State Government/U.T. Administration for identification, liberation and rehabilitation of the bonded labourer but the progress of this scheme has not been found satisfactory.

(ii) the carrying on by the State, or by a corporation owned or controlled by the State, of any trade, business, industry or service, whether to the exclusion, complete or partial, of citizens or otherwise.

RIGHTS AGAINST EXPLOITATION

Prohibition of Traffic in Human Beings and Forced Labour

23[13](1)Traffic in human beings and begar and other similar forms of forced labour are prohibited and any contravention of this provision shall be an offence punishable in accordance with law.

(2) Nothing in this article shall prevent the State from imposing compulsory service for public purposes, and in imposing such service the State shall not make any discrimination on grounds only of religion, race, caste or class or any of them.

Prohibition of Employment of Children in Factories, etc.

24. No child below the age of fourteen years shall be employed to work in any factory or mine or engaged in any other hazardous employment.

RIGHT TO FREEDOM OF RELIGION

25. Freedom of conscience and free profession, practice and propagation of religion

(1) Subject to public order, morality and health and to the other provisions of this Part, all persons are equally entitled to freedom of conscience and the right freely to process, practice and propagate religion.

(2) Nothing in this article shall affect the operation of any existing law or prevent the State from making any law.

(a) regulating or restricting any economic, financial, political or other secular activity which may be associated with religious practice;

(b) providing for social welfare and reform or the throwing open of Hindu religious institutions of a public character to all classes and sections of Hindus.

Explanation I – The wearing and carrying of Kirpans shall be deemed to be included in the profession of the Sikh religion.

Explanation II – In sub-clause (b) of clause (2), the reference to Hindus shall be construed as including a reference to persons professing the Sikh, Jaina or Buddhist religion, and the reference to Hindu religious institutions shall be construed accordingly.

26. Freedom to Manage Religious Affairs

Subject to public order, morality and health, every religious denomination or any section thereof shall have the right –

(a) to establish and maintain institutions for religious and charitable purposes;

(b) to manage its own affairs in matters of religion;

(c) to own and acquire movable and immovable property; and

(d) to administer such property in accordance with law.

27. Freedom as to Payment of Taxes for Promotion of any Particular Religion

No person shall be compelled to pay any taxes, the proceeds of which are specifically appropriated in payment of expenses for the promotion or maintenance of any particular religion or religious denomination.

28. Freedom as to Attendance at Religious instruction or Religious Worship in Certain Educational Institutions

(1) No religious instruction shall be provided in any educational wholly maintained out of State funds.

(2) Nothing in clause (1) shall apply to an educational institution which is administered by the State but has been established under any endowment or trust which requires that religious instruction shall be imparted in such institution.

(3) No person attending any educational institution recognised by the State or receiving aid out of State funds shall be required to take part in any religious instruction that may be imparted in such institution or to attend any religious worship that may be conducted in such institution or in any premises attached thereto unless such person or, if such person is a minor, his guardian has given his consent thereto.

CULTURAL AND EDUCATIONAL RIGHTS

29. Protection of Interests of Minorities

(1) Any section of the citizens residing in the territory of India or any part thereof having a distinct language, script or culture of its own shall have the right to conserve the same.

(2) No citizen shall be denied admission into any educational institution maintained by the State or receiving aid out of State funds on grounds only of religion, race, caste, language or any of them.

30. Right of Minorities to Establish and Administer Educational Institutions

(1) All minorities, whether based on religion or language, shall have the right to establish and administer educational institutions of their choice.

(1A)[14]In making any law providing for the compulsory acquisition of any property of an educational institution established and administered by a minority, referred to in clause (1), the State shall ensure that the amount fixed by or determined under such law for the acquisition of such property is such as would not restrict or abrogate the right guaranteed under that clause.

(2) The State shall not, in granting aid to educational institutions, discriminate against any educational institution on the ground that it is under the management of a minority, whether based on religion or language.

31B Validation of Certain Acts and Regulations

Without prejudice to the generality of the provisions contained in article 31A, none of the Acts and Regulations specified in the Ninth Schedule nor any of the provisions thereof shall be deemed to be void, or ever to have become void on the ground that such Act, Regulation or provision is inconsistent with, or takes away or abridges any of the rights conferred by any provision of this Part, and notwithstanding any judgement, decree or order of any court or tribunal to the contrary, each of the said Acts and Regulations shall, subject to the power of any competent Legislature to repeal or amend it, continue in force.

PART IV
DIRECTIVE PRINCIPLES OF STATE POLICY

36. Definition – In this Part, unless the context otherwise requires, "the State" has the same meaning as in Part III.

37. Application of the principles contained in this part – The provisions contained in this Part shall not be enforceable by

---

14 Clause (1A) has been inserted by the Constitution (44th Amendment) Act, 1978.

any court, but the principles therein laid down are nevertheless fundamental in the governance of the country and it shall be the duty of the State to apply these principles in making laws.

38. State to secure a social order for the promotion of welfare of the people – [14(1)][(1)] The State shall strive to promote the welfare of the people by securing and protecting as effectively as it may a social order in which justice, social, economic and political, shall inform all the institutions of the national life.

[14(2)][(2) The State shall, in particular, strive to minimise the inequalities in income, and endeavour to eliminate inequalities in status, facilities and opportunities, not only amongst individuals but also amongst groups of people residing in different areas or engaged in different vocations.]

39. Certain principles of policy to be followed by the State – The State shall, in particular, direct its policy towards securing –

(a) that the citizen, men and women equally, have the right to an adequate means of livelihood;

(b) that the ownership and control of the material resources of the community are so distributed as best to subserve the common good;

(c) that the operation of the economic system does not result in the concentration of wealth and means of production to the common detriment;

(d) that there is equal pay for equal work for both men and women;

(e) that the health and strength of workers, men and women, and the tender age of children are not abused and

---

14(1) Art. 38 renumbered as cl. (1) thereof by the Constitution (Forty-fourth Amendment) Act, 1978, s.9 (w.e.f. 20.6.1979).

14(2) Ins. by s.9, *ibid.* (w.e.f. 20.6.1979)

that citizens are not forced by economic necessity to enter avocations unsuited to their age or strength;

[14(3)][(f) that children are given opportunities and facilities to develop in a healthy manner and in conditions of freedom and dignity and that childhood and youth are protected against exploitation and against moral and material abandonment.]

39A[15] Equal Justice and Free Legal Aid

The State shall secure that the operation of the legal system promotes justice, on the basis of equal opportunity, and shall, in particular, provide free legal aid, by suitable legislation or schemes or in any other way, to ensure that opportunities for securing justice are not denied to any citizen by reason of economic or other disabilities.

45. Provision for Free and Compulsory Education for Children

The State shall endeavour to provide, within a period of ten years from the commencement of this Constitution, for free and compulsory education for all children until they complete the age of fourteen years.

46. Promotion of Educational and Economic Interests of Scheduled Castes, Scheduled Tribes and Other Weaker Sections

The State shall promote with special care the educational and economic interests of the weaker sections of the people, and in particular, of the Scheduled Castes and the Scheduled Tribes, and shall protect them from social injustice and all forms of exploitation.[16]

14(3) Subs. by the Constitution (Forty-second Amendment) Act, 1976, s.7, for cl. (f) (w.e.f. 3.1.1977).

15. Inserted by Constitution (42nd Amendment) Act, 1976.

16. Following essentially the policy as laid down under this article, welfare measures for ameliorating the socio-economic conditions of these

(*Contd.*)

PART VI

OTHER PROVISIONS AS TO MINISTERS

164(1)The Chief Minister shall be appointed by the Governor and the other Ministers shall be appointed by the Governor on the advice of the Chief Minister, and the Ministers shall hold office during the pleasure of the Governor;

---

communities have been undertaken during the successive plans. The strategy for integrated development of Scheduled Tribes through the Tribal Sub-Plan concept was adopted during the Fifth Five Year Plan. The Tribal sub-plan area is divided into 195 operational units termed as Integrated Tribal Development Project (ITDP), 25 Modified Area Development Approach (MADA), and 75 Primitive Tribal Groups. In addition 79 clusters with a total population of 5000 of which 50% are Scheduled Tribes in each cluster and 75 Primitive Tribal Groups (PTGs) have been identified. In Sixth Five Year Plan a new strategy for the rapid development of Scheduled Castes has been adopted through the mechanism of Special Component Plan, Special Central Assistance and the Scheduled Caste Development Corporations. While SCP and TSP ensure flow of funds for the development of these communities from all divisible programmes under each sector of development with specific targets as to the number of families and bastis which are to be benefited from these programmes, the Special Central Assistance is an additive to the State Plan and programmes for SC & ST for income generating schemes for economic development including directly relevant back-up services, training and institutional build-up. The total no. of SC families economically assisted under SCP from 1992-93 to 1996-97 was 117,96,986. In the case of Scheduled Tribes the SCA can be used for building infrastructure facilities also. The Scheduled Caste Development Corporations provide margin money loan to the Scheduled Caste families to benefit from the various family oriented developmental programmes, specially in the matter of securing credit. Besides this, there are a number of Centrally Sponsored Schemes which have been undertaken for the benefit of Scheduled Castes and Scheduled Tribes. Apart from these, some schemes under the non-plan sector have also been undertaken by the Central and the State Governments for the advancement of these communities. (*Source*: Annual Report of the Ministry of Social Justice and Empowerment for 1997-98)

Provided that in the States of Bihar, Madhya Pradesh and Orissa, there shall be a Minister in charge of tribal welfare who may in addition be in charge of the welfare of the Scheduled Castes and Backward Classes or any other work.

PART X

THE SCHEDULED AND TRIBAL AREAS

Administration of Scheduled Areas and Tribal Areas

244[17](1) The provisions of the Fifth Schedule shall apply to the administration and control of the Scheduled Areas and Scheduled Tribes in any State other than the States of Assam, Meghalaya, Tripura[18] and Mizoram[19].

(2) The provisions of the Sixth Schedule shall apply to the administration of the tribal areas in the States of Assam, Meghalaya, Tripura and Mizoram.

Formation of an Autonomous State comprising Certain Tribal Areas in Assam and Creation of Local Legislature or Council of Ministers or both therefor

244A (1) Notwithstanding anything in this Constitution, Parliament may, by law, form within the State of Assam an autonomous State comprising (whether wholly or in part) all or any of the tribal area specified in Part I of the table appended to paragraph 20 of the Sixth Schedule and create therefor:

(a) a body, whether elected or partly nominated, to function as a Legislature for the autonomous State, or

---

17. Scheduled Areas have been declared in the States of Andhra Pradesh, Bihar, Gujarat, Himachal Pradesh, Madhya Pradesh, Maharashtra, Orissa and Rajasthan.
18. The Constitution (Forty-ninth Amendment) Act, 1984.
19. The Fifth Schedule to the Constitution (Amendment) Act, 1976.

(b) A Council of Ministers, or both with such Constitution, powers and functions, in each case, as may be specified in the law.

(2) Any such law as is referred to in clause (1) may, in particular:

(a) specify the matters enumerated in the State List or the Concurrent List with respect to which the Legislature of the autonomous State shall have power to make laws for the whole or any part thereof, whether to the exclusion of the Legislature of the State of Assam or otherwise;
(b) define the matters with respect to which the executive power of the autonomous State shall extend;
(c) provide that any tax levied by the State of Assam shall be assigned to the autonomous State insofar as the proceeds thereof are attributable to the autonomous State;
(d) provide that any reference to a State in any article of this Constitution shall be construed as including a reference to the autonomous State; and
(e) make such supplemental, incidental and consequential provisions as may be deemed necessary.

(3) An amendment of any such law as aforesaid in so far as such amendment relates to any of the matters specified in sub-clause (a) or sub-clause (b) of clause (2) shall have no effect unless the amendment is passed in each House of Parliament by not less than two thirds of the members present and voting.

(4) Any such law as is referred to in this article shall not be deemed to be an amendment of this Constitution for the purposes of article 368 notwithstanding that it contains any provisions which amends or has the effect of amending this Constitution.

PART XII

FINANCE, PROPERTY, CONTRACTS AND SUITS

CHAPTER – I: FINANCE

Grants from the Union to Certain States

275 (1) Such sums as Parliament may by law provide shall be charged on the Consolidated Funds of India in each year as grants-in-aid of the revenues of such States as Parliament may determine to be in need of assistance, and different sums may be fixed for different States.

Provided that there shall be paid out of the Consolidated Fund of India as grants-in-aid of the revenues of a State such capital and recurring sums as may be necessary to enable that State to meet the costs of such schemes of development as may be undertaken by the States with the approval of the Government of India for the purpose of promoting the welfare of the Scheduled Tribes in that State or raising the level of administration of the Scheduled Areas therein to that of the administration of the rest of the areas of that State.

Provided further that there shall be paid out of the Consolidated Funds of India as grants-in-aid of the revenues of the State of Assam sums, capital and recurring, equivalent to:

(a) the average excess of expenditure over the revenues during the two years immediately proceeding the commencement of this Constitution in respect of the administration of the tribal areas specified in Part I of the table appended to paragraph 20 of the Sixth Schedule, and

(b) the costs of such schemes of development as may be undertaken by that State with the approval of the Government of India for the purpose of raising the level of administration of the said areas to that of the Administration of rest of the areas of that State.

(1A) On and from the formation of the autonomous State under article 244A:

(i) any sums payable under clause (a) of the second provision to clause (1) shall, if the autonomous State comprises all the tribal areas referred to therein, be paid to the autonomous State, and, if the autonomous State comprises only some of those tribal areas, be apportioned between the State of Assam and the autonomous State as the President may, by order, specify;

(ii) there shall be paid out of the Consolidated Funds of India as grants-in-aid of the revenues of the autonomous State sums, capital and recurring, equivalent to the costs of such schemes of development as may be undertaken by the autonomous State with the approval of the Government of India for the purpose of raising the level of administration of that State to that of the administration of the rest of the State of Assam.

(2) Until provision is made by Parliament under clause (1), the powers conferred on Parliament under the clause shall be exercisable by the President by order and any order made by the President under this clause shall have effect subject to any provision so made by Parliament.

Provided that after a Finance Commission has been constituted no order shall be made under this clause by the President except after considering the recommendations of the Finance Commission.

320. Functions of Public Service Commissions

(1) It shall be the duty of the Union and the State Public Service Commissions to conduct examinations for appointment to the services of the Union and the services of the State respectively.

(2) It shall also be the duty of the Union Public Service Commission, if requested by any two or more States so to do, to assist those States in framing and operating schemes of joint recruitment for any services for which candidates possessing special qualifications are required.

(3) The Union Public Service Commission or the State Public Service Commission, as the case may be, shall be consulted–

(a) on all matters relating to methods of recruitment to civil services and for civil posts;

(b) on the principles to be followed in making appointments to civil services and posts and in making promotions and transfers from one service to another and on the suitability of candidates for such appointments, promotions or transfers;

(c) on all disciplinary matters affecting a person serving under the Government of India or the Government of a State in a civic capacity, including memorials or petitions relating to such matters;

(d) on any claim by or in respect of a person who is serving or has served under the Government of India or the Government of a State or under the Crown in India or under the Government of an Indian State, in a civil capacity, that any costs incurred by him in defending legal proceedings instituted against him in respect of acts done or purporting to be done in the execution of his duty should be paid out of the Consolidated Fund of India, or, as the case may be, out of the Consolidated Fund of the State;

(e) on any claim for the award of a pension in respect of injuries sustained by a person while serving under the Government of India or the Government of a State or under the Crown in India or under the Government of an Indian State, in a civil capacity, and any question as to the amount of any such award, and it shall be the duty of the Public Service Commission to advise on any matter so referred to them and on any other matter which the President, or, as the case may be, the Governor*** of the State, may refer to them:

Provided that the President as respects the all-India services and also as respects other services and posts in connection with the affairs of the Union, and the Governor***, as respects other services and posts in connection with the affairs of a State, may make regulations specifying the matters in which either generally, or in any particular class of case or in any particular circumstances, it shall not be necessary for a Public Service Commission to be consulted.

(4) Nothing in clause (3) shall require a Public Service Commission to be consulted as respects the manner in which any provision referred to in clause (4) of article 16 may be made or as respects the manner in which effect may be given to the provisions of article 335.

(5) All regulations made under the proviso to clause (3) by the President or the Governor*** of a State shall be laid for not less than fourteen days before each House of Parliament or the House or each House of the legislature of the State, as the case may be, as soon as possible after they are made and shall be subject to such modifications, whether by way of repeal or amendment, as both Houses of Parliament or the House or both Houses of the Legislature of the State may make during the session in which they are so laid.

PART XVI

SPECIAL PROVISIONS RELATING TO CERTAIN CLASSES

Reservation of Seats for Scheduled Castes and Scheduled Tribes in the House of the People

330 (1) Seats shall be reserved in the House of the People for:

(a) the Scheduled Castes;

(b) the Scheduled Tribes except the Scheduled Tribes

in the Autonomous districts of Assam; and[1]

(c) the Scheduled Tribes in the autonomous districts of Assam.

(2) The number of seats reserved in any 'State[2] or Union Territory'[2] for the Scheduled Castes or the Scheduled Tribes under clause (1) shall bear, as nearly as may be, the same proportion to the total number of seats allotted to that State or Union Territory[2] in the House of the People as the population of the Scheduled Castes in the State or Union territory or of the Scheduled Tribes in the State or Union territory or part of the State or Union Territory[2] as the case may be, in respect of which seats are so reserved, bears to the total population of the State or Union territory[2].

(3)[3] Notwithstanding anything contained in clause (2), the number of seats reserved in the House of the People for the Scheduled Tribes in the autonomous districts of Assam shall bear to the total number of seats allotted to that State a proportion not less than the population of the Scheduled Tribes in the said autonomous districts bears to the total population of the State[3].

Explanation: In this Article and in Article 332, the expression "population" means the population as ascertained at the last preceding census of which the relevant figures have been published[4].

Provided that the reference in this Explanation to the last preceding census of which the relevant figures have been published shall, until the relevant figures for the first census taken after the year 2000 have been published, be construed as reference to the 1971 census.[4]

---

1. Substituted by the Constitution (51st Amendment) Act, 1984.
2. Inserted by the Constitution (7th Amendment) Act, 1956.
3. Inserted by the Constitution (31st Amendment) Act, 1973.
4. Inserted by the Constitution (42nd Amendment) Act, 1976.

Representation of the Anglo-Indian Community in the House of the People

331. Notwithstanding anything in Article 81, the President may, if he is of opinion that the Anglo-Indian community is not adequately represented in the House of the People, nominate not more than two members of that community to the House of the People.

Reservation of Seats for Scheduled Castes and Scheduled Tribes

332(1)[10] Seats shall be reserved for the Scheduled Castes and the Scheduled Tribes[3], except Scheduled Tribes[1] in the autonomous districts of Assam, in the Legislative Assembly of every State...

(2) Seats shall be reserved also for the autonomous districts in the Legislative Assembly of the State of Assam.

(3) The number of seats reserved for the Scheduled Castes or the Scheduled Tribes in the Legislative Assembly of any State under clause (1) shall bear, as nearly as may be, the same proportion to the total number of seats in the Assembly as the population of the Scheduled Castes in the State or of the Scheduled Tribes in the State or part of the State, as the case may be, in respect of which seats are so reserved, bears to the total population of the State.

---

5. Effect of reservation.
   (a) The effect of reservation of seats for the Scheduled Castes and Scheduled Tribes, is to guarantee a minimum number of seats to the members of the Scheduled Castes and Scheduled Tribes. It does not deprive a member of a Scheduled Castes or Scheduled Tribes of his right to contest a general seat on the strength of the very nomination for a reserved seat.
   (b) If, in a two-member constituency, one seat is reserved for the Scheduled Castes, and, besides the member returned to his reserved seat, another member of the Scheduled Castes secures the highest votes at the general election, there is nothing to prevent the second member of the Scheduled Castes from being elected to the second seat.
6. The words 'specific in Part A... First Schedule' were omitted by the Constitution (7th Amendment) Act, 1956.

(3A)[7] Notwithstanding anything contained in clause (3), until the taking effect, under article 170, of the re-adjustment, on the basis of the first census after the year 2000, of the number of seats in the Legislative Assemblies of the States of Arunachal Pradesh, Meghalaya, Mizoram and Nagaland, the seats which shall be reserved for the Scheduled Tribes in the Legislative Assembly of any such State shall be:

(a) If all the seats in the Legislative Assembly of such State in existence on the date of coming into force of the Constitution (Fifty-Seventh Amendment) Act, 1987 (hereafter in this clause referred to as the existing Assembly) are held by members of the Scheduled Tribes, all the seats except one.

(b) In any other case, such number of seats as bears to the total number of seats, a proportion not less than the number (as on the said date) of members belonging to the Scheduled Tribes in the existing Assembly bears to the total number of seats in the existing Assembly.

(3B) Notwithstanding anything contained in clause (3), until the re-adjustment, under article, takes effect on the basis of the first census after the year 2000, of the number of seats in the Legislative Assembly of the State of Tripura, the seats which shall be reserved for the Scheduled Tribes in the Legislative Assembly shall be, such number of seats as bears to the total number of seats, a proportion not less than the number, as on the date of coming into force of the Constitution (72nd Amendment) Act, 1992, of members belonging to the Scheduled Tribes in the Legislative Assembly in existence on the said date bears to the total number of seats in that Assembly).[8]

---

7. Sub-sec. (3A) has been inserted by the Constitution (57th Amendment) Act, 1987

8. Clause (3B) has been inserted in Art. 332 by the Constitution (72nd) Amendment) Act, 1992, w.e.f 5-12-1992.

(4) The number of Seats reserved for an autonomous districts in the Legislative Assembly of the State of Assam shall bear to the total population of the State.

(5) The constituencies for the seats reserved for any autonomous district of Assam shall not comprise any area outside the district....[9]

(6) No person who is a member of a Scheduled Tribe of any autonomous district of the State of Assam shall be eligible for election of the Legislative Assembly of the State from any constituency of that district...[9]

Representation of the Anglo-Indian Community in the Legislative Assemblies of the States

333. Notwithstanding anything in article 170, the Governor... of a State may, if he is of opinion that the Anglo-Indian community needs representation in the Legislative Assembly of the State and is not adequately represented therein, nominate one member of the community to the Assembly.[11]

Representation of Seats and Special Representation to Cease after Fifty Years

334. Notwithstanding anything in the foregoing provisions of this Part, the provisions of this Constitution relating to:

(a) the reservation of seats for the Scheduled Castes and the Scheduled Tribes in the House of the People and in the Legislative Assemblies of the State; and

(b) the representation of the Anglo-Indian community in the House of the People and in the Legislative Assemblies of the States by nomination, shall cease

---

9. Certain words omitted by the North-Eastern Areas (Reorganisation) Act, 1971 (81 of 1971), s. 71 (w.e.f. 21.1.72)

10. The reservation of seats provided under Art. 332 cannot be challenged on the ground of denial of right guaranteed under Art. 14.

11. Substituted by Constitution (23rd Amendment) Act, 1969.

to have effect on the expiration of a period of *fifty*[12] years from the commencement of this Constitution.

(b) the representation of the Anglo-Indian community in the House of the People and in the Legislative Assemblies of the States by nomination, shall cease to have effect on the expiration of a period of *fifty*[12] years from the commencement of this Constitution.

Provided that nothing in this article shall affect any representation in the House of the People or in the Legislative Assembly of a State until the dissolution of the then existing House or Assembly, as the case may be.

Claims of Scheduled Castes and Scheduled Tribes to Services and Posts

335. The claim of the members of the Scheduled Castes and the Scheduled Tribes shall be taken into consideration, consistently with the maintenance of efficiency of administration, in the making of appointments to the services and posts in connection with the affairs of the Union or of a State.[13]

---

12. The word 'twenty' was subs. by the Constitution (8th Amendment) Act, 1959, for "ten years", again by the word 'thirty', by the Constitution (23rd Amendment) Act, 1969, w.e.f. 23.1.1970, again by the word 'forty', by the Constitution (45th Amendment) Act, 1969, w.e.f. 23.1.1970, again, by the word 'fifty' by the Constitution (62nd Amendment) Act, 1989.
13. It is the constitutional duty of the State to take into consideration the claims of the members of the Scheduled Castes and Scheduled Tribes in the matter of appointment (subject, of course, to the consideration of the efficiency of the administration). This duty is to be exercised in keeping with the Directive Principles laid down in Art. 46 to promote with special care the educational and economic interests of the Scheduled Castes and Scheduled Tribes, and to protect them from social injustice and all forms of exploitation.

Special Provision for Anglo-Indian Community in Certain Services

336[14](1) During the first two years after the commencement of this Constitution, appointments of members of the Anglo-Indian community to posts in the railway, customs, postal and telegraph services of the Union shall be made on the same basis as immediately before the fifteenth day of August, 1947.

During every succeeding period of two years, the number of posts reserved for the members of the said community in the said services shall, as nearly as possible, be less by ten per cent than the numbers so reserved during the immediately preceding period of two years:

Provided that at the end of ten years from the commencement of this Constitution all such reservations shall cease.

(2) Nothing in clause (1) shall bar the appointment of members of the Anglo-Indian community to posts other than, or in addition to, those reserved for the community under that clause if such members are found qualified for appointment on merit as compared with the members of other communities.

Special Provision with Respect to Educational Grants for the benefit of Anglo-Indian Community

337. During the first three financial years after the commencement of this Constitution, the same grants, if any, shall be made by

---

14. Since Art. 336 and 337 were not amended by the Constitution (8th Amendment) Act, 1959, the reservations in favour of the Anglo-Indian have ceased to operate at the end of January 25, 1960. The period stipulated in Art. 337 having expired, this Article has ceased to be operative and there is no longer any constitutional right of Anglo-Indian educational institutions to receive special protection.

the Union and by each State...[15] for the benefit to the Anglo-Indian community in respect of education as were made in the financial year ending on the thirty-first day of March, 1948.

During every succeeding period of three years the grants may be less by ten per cent than those for the immediately preceding period of three years.

Provided that at the end of ten years from the commencement of this Constitution such grants to the extent to which they are a special concession to the Anglo-Indian community, shall cease:

Provided further that no educational institution shall be entitled to receive any grant under this article unless at least forty per cent of the annual admissions therein are made available to members of communities other than the Anglo-Indian community.

National Commission for Scheduled Castes and Scheduled Tribes

338[16](1) There shall be a Commission for the Scheduled Castes and Scheduled Tribes to be known as the National Commission for the Scheduled Castes and Scheduled Tribes.

(2) Subject to the provisions of any law made in this behalf by Parliament, the Commission shall consist of a Chairperson, Vice-Chairperson and five other Members and the conditions of service and tenure of office of the Chairperson, Vice-Chairperson and other Members shall be such as the President may by rule determine.

(3) The Chairperson, Vice-Chairperson and other Members of the Commission shall be appointed by the President by warrant under his hand and seal.

(4) The Commission shall have the power to regulate its own procedure.

---

15. The words 'specified in Part A... Schedule' were omitted by the Constitution (7th Amendment) Act, 1956.

16. Substituted by the Constitution (65th Amendment) Act, 1990. Originally article 338 of the Constitution provided for a Special Officer for the

(*Contd.*)

(5) It shall be duty of the Commission:

(a) to investigate and monitor all matters relating to the safeguards provided for the Scheduled Castes and Scheduled Tribes under this Constitution or under any other law for the time being in force or under any order of the Government and to evaluate the working of such safeguards;

(b) to inquire into specific complaints with respect to the deprivation of rights and safeguards of the Scheduled Castes and Scheduled Tribes;

(c) to participate and advice on the planning process of socio-economic development of the Scheduled Castes and Scheduled Tribes and to evaluate the progress of their development under the Union and any State;

(d) to present to the President, annually and at such other times as the Commission may deem fit, reports upon the working of those safeguards;

(e) to make in such reports recommendations as to the measures that should be taken by the Union or any State for the effective implementing of those safeguards

---

Scheduled Castes and Scheduled Tribes to investigate all matters relating to the safeguards provided for the Scheduled Castes and Scheduled Tribes under the Constitution and to report to the President on their working. It was felt that a high level five-member Commission under Art. 338 will be a more effective arrangement in respect of the constitutional safeguards for Scheduled Castes and Scheduled Tribes than a single Special Officer. It was also felt that it was necessary to elaborate the functions of the said Commission so as to cover measures that should be taken by the Union or any State for the effective implementation of those safeguards and other measures for the protection, welfare and socio-economic development of the Scheduled Castes and Scheduled Tribes and to entrust to the Commission such other functions in relation to the protection, welfare and development and advancement of the Scheduled Castes and Scheduled Tribes as the President may decide, subject to any law made by Parliament and the Legislature of the States. The first incumbent to the post of Special Officer designated as the Commissioner for Scheduled Castes and

(*Contd.*)

and other measures for the protection, welfare and socio-economic development of the Scheduled Castes and Scheduled Tribes; and

(f) to discharge such other functions in relation to the protection, welfare and development and advancement of the Scheduled Castes and Scheduled Tribes as the President may, subject to the provisions of any law made by Parliament, by rule specify.

(6) The President shall cause all such reports to be laid before each House of Parliament along with a memorandum explaining the action taken or proposed to be taken on the recommendations.[17]

(7) Where any such reports, or any part thereof, relates to any matter with which any State Government is concerned, a copy of such report shall be forwarded to the Governor of the State who shall cause it to be laid before the Legislature of the State along with a memorandum explaining the action taken or proposed to be taken on the recommendations relating to the State and the reasons for the non-acceptance, if any, of such recommendations.

(8) The Commission shall, while investigating any matter referred to in sub-clause (a) or inquiring into any sub-clause (b) of

---

Scheduled Tribes was Late Sh. L.M. Shrikant, appointed on 18th November, 1950 with 17 regional offices all over the country. The last incumbent to the post of Special Officer was Dr. B.D. Sharma. The National Commission for Scheduled Castes and Scheduled Tribes was first constituted by the Ministry of Home Affairs by an executive order in 1978 under the chairmanship of Late Shri Bhola Paswan, M.P. For quite some time both the Commissioner for Scheduled Castes and Scheduled Tribes as well as the National Commission for Scheduled Castes and Scheduled Tribes continued to function simultaneously though the statutory power under Article 338 remained with the former. This arrangement continued till 1990 when Article 338 was amended and Special Officer (designated as Commissioner for Scheduled Castes and Scheduled Tribes) was substituted by the National Commission for Scheduled Castes and Scheduled Tribes. The present Chairman of the Commission is Shri Dalip Singh Bhuria.

17. Added by the Constitution (7th Amendment) Act, 1956.

clause (5), have all the powers of a civil court trying a suit and in particular in respect of the following matters, namely:

(a) summoning and enforcing the attendance of any person from any part of India and examining him on oath;

(b) requiring the discovery and production of any document;

(c) receiving evidence on affidavits;

(d) requisitioning any public record or copy thereof from any court or office;

(e) issuing commissions for the examination of witnesses and documents;

(f) any other matter which the President may, by rule, determine

(9) The Union and every State Government shall consult the Commission on all major policy matters affecting Scheduled Castes and Scheduled Tribes.[18]

(10) In this article, references to the Scheduled Castes and Scheduled Tribes shall be construed as including reference to such other backward classes as the President may, on receipt of the report of a Commission appointed under clause (1) of article 340, by order specify and also to the Anglo-Indian community.[19]

Control of the Union over the Administration of Scheduled Areas and the Welfare of Scheduled Tribes

339[20](1) The President may at any time and shall, at the expiration

---

18. The words 'specified in Part A... Schedule' were omitted by *ibid.*
19. The words 'or Rajpramukh' was omitted by *ibid.*
20. In pursuance of the provisions of this Article, a Commission was appointed by the President of India under the designation. the Scheduled Areas and Scheduled Tribes Commission on the 28th April, 1960 under the Chairmanship of Late Sh. U.N. Dhebar which submitted its report to the Govt. of India on October 14, 1961.

of ten years from the commencement of this Constitution, by order appoint a Commission to report on the administration of the Scheduled Areas and the welfare of the Scheduled Castes and Scheduled Tribes in the States**.

The order may define the composition, powers and procedure of the Commission and may contain such incidental or ancillary provisions as the President may consider necessary or desirable.

(2)[21] The executive power of the Union shall extend to the giving of direction to a State as to the drawing up and execution of schemes specified in the direction to be essential for the welfare of the Scheduled Tribes in the State.

Appointment of a Commission to Investigate the Conditions of Backward Classes

340[22](1) The President may by order appoint a Commission consisting of such persons as he thinks fit to investigate the conditions of socially and educationally backward classes within the territory of India and the difficulties under which they labour and to make recommendations as

---

21. The executive power given under Art. 339 has not so far been exercised by the Union Govt.

22. The first Backward Classes Commission known as Kaka Kalelkar Commission was appointed in 1953 which submitted its report in 1955. The Second Backward Classes Commission was appointed in 1979 under the chairmanship of Late Sh. B.P. Mandal which submitted its report to the Govt. of India in 1980. The National Commission for Backward Classes Act, 1993 was enacted on the direction of the Supreme Court to set up a permanent body for entertaining, examining and recommending upon requests for inclusion and complaints of over-inclusion and under-inclusion in the lists of Other Backward Classes of citizens. As per provision of the act, the advice tendered by such body shall ordinarily be binding upon the Govt. The Commission was constituted on 14th August, 1993 and reconstituted in March 1997. The Government of India have so far specified more than 3000 communities as Other Backward Classes in various States and Union Territories.

to the steps that should be taken by the Union or any State to remove such difficulties and to improve their condition and as to the grants that should be made for the purpose by the Union or any State and the conditions subject to which such grants should be made, and the order appointing such Commission shall define the procedure to be followed by the Commission.

(2) A Commission so appointed shall investigate the matters referred to them and present to the President a report setting out the facts as found by them and making such recommendations as they think proper.

(3) The President shall cause a copy of the report so presented together with a memorandum explaining the action taken thereon to be laid before each House of Parliament.

Scheduled Castes

341(1) The President may, with respect to any State or Union territory[17], and where it is a State...[18]after consultation with the Governor...[19] thereof, by public notification, specify the castes, races or tribes or parts of or groups within castes, races or tribes which shall for the purposes of this Constitution be deemed to be Scheduled Castes in relation to the State or Union territory, as the case may be.[17]

341(1) The list of Scheduled Castes contained in the Constitution (Scheduled Castes) Order, 1950, was notified on 10.8.1950 and amended by the Scheduled Castes and Scheduled Tribes Orders (Amendment) Act, 1956 keeping in view the recommendations of the First Backward Classes Commission (1953) and the reorganisation of States. Seven Presidential Orders have so far been issued specifying the lists of Scheduled Castes in various States/Union Territories. (471 communities)

2. In order to belong to a Scheduled Caste under this Order, a person must profess to be either a Hindu or a Sikh or a Buddhist religion. The Sikh religion was added in 1956 and Buddhism in 1990.

3. Where, therefore, a person has made a public declaration that he has adopted the Christian religion, he cannot thereafter claim to be a

(*Contd.*)

(2) Parliament may by law include in or exclude from the list of Scheduled Castes specified in a notification issued under clause (1) any caste, race or tribe, or part of or group within any caste, race or tribe, but save as aforesaid a notification issued under the said clause shall not be varied by any subsequent notification.

Scheduled Caste on the ground that his conversion to Christianity was not efficacious. If, however, there is no proof of conversion to a religion other than the Hindu religion but mere acceptance, of certain ideological tenets, the person does not lose his status as a member of Scheduled Caste. Again, on re-conversion to Hinduism he can get back status as a member of Scheduled Caste, if his community has accepted him and he has got a certificate about his re-conversion to Hindu, or Sikh or Buddhist religion.

4. It would be thus observed that under Article 341 not only castes and groups within castes but also races or tribes and groups within races or tribes can be specified as Scheduled Castes. Under Article 342, however, only tribes or tribal communities or groups within tribes or tribal communities have to be specified as Scheduled Tribes. It is, therefore, clear that while tribes may be included in the schedule of castes, castes shall not be included in the schedule of tribes. Both the Articles under which the President is empowered to issue orders listing Scheduled Castes and Scheduled Tribes, have not made any reference to any religion and also not made any stipulation in that regard. Secondly, the first list of castes and tribes to be specified as the Scheduled Castes or Scheduled Tribes will be issued by a Presidential Order alone. Thirdly, the lists of Schedule Castes/Schedule Tribes will be in relation to each State/Union Territory or specific areas within it. In view of this there cannot be any all-India list of the Scheduled Castes and Scheduled Tribes. Fourthly, the lists of Scheduled Castes/Scheduled Tribes will be drawn up in consultation with the State Government/Union Territory Administration and lastly any variation in the Presidential Orders specifying the lists of Scheduled Castes and Scheduled Tribes can be made by an Act of Parliament only and not by any State Legislature or by any executive order of the Central or the State Government.

5. It is open to the President to declare that a caste or sub-caste shall be deemed to be a Scheduled Caste in a particular part of a State and not in another part. Conversely, where the President's Notification declares a caste to be a Scheduled Caste for the purposes of certain specified State, no Court can direct that caste to be declared Scheduled Caste in relation to another.

Scheduled Tribes

342(1) The President may with respect to any State or Union territory and where it is a State after consultation with the Governor thereof by public notification, specify the tribes or tribal communities or parts of or groups within tribes or tribal communities which shall for the purpose of this Constitution be deemed to be Scheduled Tribes in relation to that State or Union territory, as the case may be.

(2) Parliament may by law include in or exclude from the list of Schedule Tribes specified in a notification issued under clause (1) any tribe or tribal community or part of or group within any tribe or tribal community, but save as aforesaid a notification issued under the said clause shall not be varied by any subsequent notification.

---

6. It is not open to the Court to question the validity of the President's determination that a particular caste or tribe is a Scheduled Caste or Tribe and also of the finding of any administrative inquiry which preceded the making of the Presidential Order.
7. The reason is that the Court has no power to modify the President's order or to make any addition to it.
8. It is now established that where a person belonging to a Scheduled Caste or Scheduled Tribes of one State migrates to another State, he will not be entitled to claim the privileges or benefits (e.g. admission to an educational institution) admissible to a member of Scheduled Caste or Scheduled Tribe of the state to which he has migrated, even though there may be a Scheduled Caste or Scheduled Tribe of the same nomenclature in the latter State. Insofar as the benefits of the Central Govt. are concerned, all the Scheduled Castes/ Scheduled Tribes are entitled irrespective of the State/UT to which they belong.
9. The main criteria adopted for the inclusion of castes and communities in the list of Scheduled Castes was extreme social, educational and economic backwardness arising out of the traditional practice of untouchability since the phenomenon of untouchability was prevalent among Hindus only due to caste system which is not recognised by other religions.
10. In the caste hierarchy among the Scheduled Castes, Bhangi, Mehtar, Chura, Dom, Hela, Mazhabi etc. engaged in sweeping and scavenging are considered to be the lowest.

342 (1) The Constitution (Scheduled Tribes) Orders 1950 was notified on 6.9.1950. Nine Presidential Orders have so far been issued specifying the list of Scheduled Tribes in various States/Union Territories. (540 tribes)

(Contd.)

PART XVII

SPECIAL DIRECTIVES

Language to be used in Representations for Redress of Grievances

350 Every person shall be entitled to submit a representation for the redress of any grievance to any officer or authority of the Union or a State in any of the languages used in the Union or in the State, as the case may be.

Facilities for Instruction in Mother Tongue at Primary Stage

350A It shall be the endeavour of every State and of every local authority within the State to provide adequate facilities for instruction in the mother-tongue at the primary stage of education to children belonging to linguistic minority groups; and the President may issue such directions to any state as he considers necessary or proper for securing the provision of such facilities.

Special Officer for Linguistic Minorities

350B (1) There shall be a Special Officer for linguistic minorities to be appointed by the President.

---

2. The criteria followed for specifying Scheduled Tribes in 1950 was (a) Primitive traits, (b) Distinct culture, (c) Geographical isolation, (d) Shyness of contact with the community at large, and (e) Social, educational and economic backwardness.
3. Religion is not a bar in the case of Scheduled Tribes.
4. The position as discussed at point nos. 4, 5, 6, 7 and 8 in the case of Scheduled Castes (Art. 341) will apply to Scheduled Tribes also

350A have been inserted by the Constitution (7th Amendment) Act, 1956.

350B The Government of India has notified 5 communities namely Muslims, Sikhs, Christians, Buddhists and Zoroastrians as Minorities at the national level. As per 1991 Census population of minority groups constitutes 17.17% of the total population of the country.

(2) It shall be the duty of the Special Officer to investigate all matters relating to the safeguards provided for linguistic minorities under this Constitution and report to the President upon those matters at such intervals as the President may direct, and the President shall cause all reports to be laid before each House of Parliament and sent to the Government of the States concerned.

NATIONAL COMMISSION FOR MINORITIES

Despite the safeguards provided in the Constitution and the laws in force, there persists amongst the minorities a feeling that they are discriminated against. For preserving secular character of security and promoting communal harmony, Government of India attaches the highest importance to the enforcement of the safeguards provided for minorities. Accordingly, Government set up Minorities Commission in 1978 to act as a watch dog for monitoring the effective implementation of various Central and State laws and implementation of various programmes and policies for welfare of minorities.

In May 1992, the National Commission Minorities Act, 1992 was enacted giving statutory status to the erstwhile Minorities Commission thus making it a more effective body to safeguard interests of minorities. The National Commission of Minorities was reconstituted on 26th Nov., 1996 under the Chairmanship of Prof.(Dr.) Tahir Mahmood.

COMMISSIONER FOR LINGUISTIC MINORITIES

The Office of the Special Officer for Linguistic Minorities (commonly known as the Commissioner for Linguistic Minorities) was created in July, 1957 in pursuance of the provision of Article 350-B of the Constitution, which came into existence as a result of the recommendations of the State Reorganisation Commission. Under the said Article, it shall be the duty of the Commissioner for Linguistic Minorities to investigate all matters relating to the safeguards provided for the Linguistic Minorities under the Constitution and report to the President upon these matters at such intervals as the President may direct. The organisation of the Commissioner for Linguistic Minorities has its headquarters at Allahabad with Regional Offices at Calcutta, Belgaum and Chennai. Dr. Harbhajan Singh Deol has been appointed as Commissioner for Linguistic Minorities on 7.10.96.

15-POINT PROGRAMME FOR WELFARE OF MINORITIES

The need for promotion of communal harmony and prevention of communal violence and improvement in the socio-economic conditions of minorities was emphasised by the late Prime Minister Smt. Indira Gandhi in her letter to Chief Ministers dated May 11,1983. This letter laid the foundation for the 15-Point Programme for welfare of minorities. The programme classifies measures broadly under three categories namely safety and protection of life and property, representation in the jobs under State and Central Governments and socio-educational development. The programme envisages special consideration for minorities in recruitment of police personnel and fair and adequate share in development programmes. The Programme is being implemented by States/UTs and the concerned Central Ministries/Departments.

I. Communal Riots

1. In the areas which has been identified as communally sensitive riot prone, District and Police Official of the highest known efficiency, impartiality and secular record must be posted. In such areas and even elsewhere, the prevention of communal tension should be one of the primary duties of DM and SP. Their performance in this regard should be an important factor in determining the promotion prospects.
2. Good work done in this regard by District and Police Officials should be rewarded.
3. Severe action should be taken against all those who incite communal tension or take part in violence.
4. Special court or courts specifically earmarked to try communal offences should be set up so that offenders are brought to book speedily.
5. Victims of communal riots should be given immediate relief and provided prompt and adequate financial assistance for the rehabilitation.
6. Radio & TV must also help in restoring confidence, communal harmony and peace in such affected areas.
7. It is unfortunate that certain sections of the press sometimes indulge in the tendentious reporting and publication of objectionable and inflammatory material which may incite communal tension. Editors, printers, publishers and other concerned will co-operate in finding a way to avoid publication of such material.

II. Recruitment to State and Central Services

8. In the recruitment of police personnel, State Governments should be advised to give special consideration to minorities. For this purpose, the composition of selection communities should be representative.

9. The Central Government should take similar action in the recruitment of personnel to the Central Police Forces.
10. Large scale employment opportunities are provided by the Railways, Nationalised Banks and Public Sector Enterprises. In these cases also the concerned departments would ensure that special consideration is given to recruitment from minority communities.
11. In many areas recruitment is done through competitive examination. Often minority groups have been handicapped in taking advantage of the education system to complete on equal terms in such examination. To help them to overcome these handicaps step should be taken to encourage the starting of coaching classes in minority educational institutions to train persons to compete successfully in these examinations.
12. The acquisition of technical skills by those minorities who are today lagging behind would also in national development arrangements should be made to set up ITIs and polytechnics by Government or private agencies in predominantly minority areas encourage admission in such institutions of adequate number of persons belonging to these communities.

III. Other Measures

13. In various development programmes including the 20-Point Programme, care should be taken to see that minorities secure a fair and adequate measure that benefits flowing therefrom. In the various committees which are set up to oversee the implementation of such programmes, members of these communities should be actively involved.
14. Apart from the above general issues there are various local problems which develop into needless irritants to minorities. For instant encroachment of wakf properties and on graveyards have led to protests and grievances in some places. Suitable steps should be taken to deal with such problems on an expeditious and satisfactory basis.
15. Problems relating to minorities need to be attended to on a continuing basis so that apprehensions are allayed and genuine grievances redressed. To facilitate this, a special cell will be created in the Ministry of Home Affairs to deal with matters relating to minority.

Concrete Measures taken by the concerned Ministries/Deptt.

(i) The Ministry of Home Affairs has set up Rapid Action Force charged with the special task of quelling communal riots. Guidelines have been issued to State Govts. and measures for prevention of riots, dealing with situation arising out of riots and providing relief and rehabilitation to the riots victims. The guidelines for promotion of communal harmony issued to State Govts. in 1990 by Ministry of Home Affairs grant in

---

case of death or permanent incapacitation from Rs. 20,000 to Rs. 50,000 and also a pension of Rs. 500 per month to widows of riots victims in the low income group. Most of the States have accepted these guidelines. In 1992, Ministry of Home Affairs suggested that on a uniform scale the next of the kin of persons killed in riots be paid Rs. one lakh and those who are permanently incapacitated Rs. 50,000. However, in the context of riots which took place in the wake of Ayodhya incident, special dispensation has been made for payment of ex-gratia relief of Rs. 2 lakhs as a one time exception. It was also suggested that assistance such as employment to the widows, allotment of house site and bank loans to the other riot victims should also be made. There is a provision for assistance to the children of families affected by communal violence under National Foundation for Communal Harmony set up under the Ministry of Home Affairs which includes education and vocational training to these children. State Govts. are also advised to set up Special Courts to try communal offences expeditiously. The total number of such courts constituted so far is 22.

(ii) The Ministry of Information and Broadcasting commissioned features highlighting mutual co-operation between majority and minority communities during communal riots and special programmes focussing on promotion of communal harmony.

(iii) The Deptt. of Education (Ministry of Human Resource Development) started programmes of educational development in 41 identified districts in the country with minority concentration. An Area Intensive Programme in 11 States, namely Uttar Pradesh (13), West Bengal (9), Kerala (5), Bihar (3), Karnataka (3), Maharashtra (2), Andhra Pradesh (2) and one each in Haryana, Madhya Pradesh, Rajasthan and Gujarat is being implemented at the block level of these 41 identified districts to provide basic education infrastructure and facilities. Under this scheme 100% assistance is given by the Central Government.

The Department of Education has also introduced a scheme to provide financial assistance for modernisation of Madrasa Education and for teaching of Science, Mathematics, Social Studies and languages in traditional institution Madrasas/Maktabs on a voluntary basis. Under this scheme also 100% grant is given by the Central Government.

These 41 districts are also covered under the Scheme of Community Polytechnics to impart technical skills to eligible persons belonging to minority communities.

(iv) The Ministry of Labour had also set up 280 ITIs in 19 out of these 41 districts and trades relevant for minority artisans and workers are introduced in these institutes. Director General, Employment and Training, Ministry of Labour also issued instructions to State Governments to ensure that there`is no discrimination in matters of registration and sponsoring of minority candidates for vocational training courses.

(v) The Ministry of Welfare set up an apex financial corporation, namely National Minorities Development and Finance Corporation (NMDFC) with an authorised capital of Rs. 500 crores for providing concessional finance to eligible minority beneficiaries for setting up self-employment ventures. Government of India's contribution to the equity of NMDFC is restricted to 25% of the paid up share capital which has been raised to 60% i.e. Rs. 300 crores of the share capital of the Corporation, subject to pro-rata contribution by the State Govt./UT. Administrations. The balance will be held by the State Governments/Corporation and individuals.

(vi) The Ministry of Industries is implementing special programmes for rural artisans under Khadi and Village Industries in minority concentration districts through State level KVICs. Ministry of Rural Development Department is implementing IRDP/TRYSEM/JRY programmes through the State Government concerned.

(vii) The Department of Small Scale Industries and Agro-Rural Industries are implementing the PM's Rozgar Yojana Scheme all over the country for entrepreneurial skills among selected candidates. The training is conducted through District Industry Centres. The erstwhile Scheme of Self-employment for Educated Unemployed Youth was merged with the PM's Rozgar Yojana Scheme in April, 1994.

(viii) The Reserve Bank of India has been requested to identify areas in minority concentration districts where new branches can be opened to augment flow of credit to the minorities.

(ix) Department of Personnel and Training has issued instructions making it mandatory for all recruiting authorities of Central Government and Public Sector Undertakings to have one member belonging to SCs/STs and one member belonging to minority community in the Selection Boards/ Committees constituted for making recruitment to 10 or more vacancies in the Group C & D posts/services.

Those sections of minorities which have been included in the OBCs list are eligible to take advantages of reservation provisions in the Civil Services and posts under Government of India at par with other OBC candidates.

(x) The Ministry of Welfare has been operating a scheme of pre-examination coaching for weaker sections among minorities and other backward classes to enable them to compete on equal terms with other candidates in competitive examinations for various jobs. The scheme is being implemented through institutions of repute. Since its inception in 1992-93, the scheme has covered 197 institutions where 10,840 candidates have been coached for various competitive examinations. A similar scheme is being implemented by University Grants Commission in 21 Universities and 32 colleges. (*Source*: Annual Report of the Ministry of Social Justice and Empowerment for 1997-98)

PART XIX

366. Definitions – In this Constitution, unless the context otherwise requires, the following expressions have the meanings hereby respectively assigned to them, that is to say:

(2)[66] An "Anglo-Indian" means a person whose father or any of whose other male progenitors in the male line is or was European descent but who is domiciled within the territory of India and is or was born within such territory of parents habitually resident therein and not established there for temporary purposes only;

24. "Scheduled Castes" means such castes, races or tribes or parts of or groups within such castes, races or tribes as are deemed under article 341 to be Scheduled Castes for the purposes of this Constitution.

25. "Scheduled Tribes" means such tribes or tribal communities or parts of or groups within such tribes or tribal communities as are deemed under article 342 to be Scheduled Tribes for the purposes of this Constitution.

PART XXI

Special Provisions with respect to the State of Nagaland

371A*Notwithstanding anything in this Constitution–

(a) no Act of Parliament in respect of:

(i) religious or social practices of the Nagas;

(ii) Naga Customary law and procedure;

(iii) administration of civil and criminal justice involving decisions according to Naga customary law;

Inserted by the Constitution (13th Amendment) Act, 1962.

(iv) ownership and transfer of land and its resources, shall apply to the State of Nagaland unless the Legislative Assembly of Nagaland by a resolution so decides.

(b) the Governor of Nagaland shall have special responsibility with respect to law and order in the State of Nagaland for so long as in his opinion internal disturbances occurring in the Naga Hills-Tuensang Area immediately before the formation of that State continue therein or in any part thereof and in the discharge of his functions in relation thereto the Governor shall, after consulting the Council of Ministers, exercise his individual judgement as to the action to be taken:

Provided that if any question arises whether any matter is or is not a matter as respects which the Governor is under the sub-clause required to act in the exercise of his individual judgement the decision of the Governor in his discretion shall be final, and the validity of anything done by the Governor shall not be called in question on the ground that he ought or ought not to have acted in the exercise of his individual judgement:

Provided further that if the President on receipt of a report from the Governor or otherwise is satisfied that it is no longer necessary for the Governor to have special responsibility with respect to law and order in the State of Nagaland, he may by order direct that the Governor shall cease to have such responsibility with effect from such date as may be specified in the order.

(c) in making his recommendation with respect to any demand for a grant, the Governor of Nagaland shall ensure that any money provided by the Government of India out of the Consolidated Fund of India for any specific service or purpose is included in the demand for a grant relating to that service or purpose and not in any other demand;

(d) as from such date as the Governor of Nagaland may by public notification in this behalf specify there shall be established a regional council for the Tuensang district consisting of thirty-five members and the Governor shall in his discretion make rules providing for–

(i) the composition of the regional council and the manner in which the members of the regional council shall be chosen:

Provided that the Deputy Commissioner of the Tuensang district shall be the Chairman ex-officio of the regional council and the Vice-Chairman of the regional council shall be elected by the members thereof from amongst themselves:

(ii) the qualifications for being chosen as, and for being, members of the regional council;

(iii) the term of office of, and the salaries and allowances, if any, to be paid to members of the regional council;

(iv) the procedure and conduct of business of the regional council;

(v) the appointment of officers and staff of the regional council and their conditions of service; and

(vi) any other matter in respect of which it is necessary to make rules for the constitution and proper functioning of the regional council.

*(2) Notwithstanding anything in this Constitution, for a period of ten years from the date of the formation of the State of

---

* Paragraph 2 of the Constitution (Removal of Difficulties) Order No. X provides that Art. 371A of the Constitution of India shall have effect as if the following proviso were added to paragraph (i) of sub-Cl. (e) of Cl (2) thereof, namely:-

Nagaland or for such further period as the Governor may, on the recommendation of the regional council, by public notification, specify in this behalf-

(a) the administration of the Tuensang district shall be carried on by the Governor:

(b) where any money is provided by the Government of India to the Government of Nagaland to meet the requirements of the State of Nagaland as a whole, the Governor shall in his discretion arrange for an equitable allocation of that money between the Tuensang and the rest of the State:

(c) no Act of the Legislature of Nagaland shall apply to the Tuensang district unless the Governor, on the recommendation of the regional council, by public notification so directs and the Governor in giving such direction with respect to any such Act may direct that the Act shall in its application to the Tuensang district or any part thereof have effect subject to such exceptions or modifications as the Governor may specify on the recommendation of the regional council:

Provided that any direction given under this sub-clause may be given so as to have retrospective effect;

(d) the Governor may make regulations for the peace, progress and good government of the Tuensang district and any regulations so made may repeal or amend with retrospective effect, if necessary, any Act of Parliament or any other law which is for the time being applicable to that district;

"Provided that the Governor may, on the advice of the Chief Minister, appoint any person as Minister for Tuensang Affairs to act as such until such time as persons are chosen in accordance with law to fill the seats allocated to the Tuensang district in the Legislative Assembly of Nagaland."

(e) (i) one of the members representing the Tuensang district in the Legislative Assembly of Nagaland shall be appointed Minister for Tuensang affairs by the Governor on the advice of the Chief Minister and the Chief Minister in tendering his advice shall act on the recommendation of the majority of the members as aforesaid;

(ii) the Minister for Tuensang affairs shall deal with, and have direct access to the Governor on all matters relating to the Tuensang district but he shall keep the Chief Minister informed about the same;

In July 1960, an agreement was reached by the Government of India with the leaders of Naga People Convention under which it was decided that Naga Hills - Tuensang Areas (Nagaland), which was then a part 'B' Tribal Area within the State of Assam, would be formed into a separate state in the Union of India.

The agreement *inter alia* provided that-

(a) The Governor of the State of Nagaland would have special responsibility for law and order for so long as the law and order situation continued to remain disturbed on account of hostile activities;

(b) The Governor would have general responsibility with regard to the funds made available to the new State by the Government of India;

(c) The administration of the Tuensang district of Nagaland would be carried on by the Governor for a period of ten years during which it is expected that the people of that area would be in a position to shoulder fuller responsibilities of administration. A Regional Council is to be formed for the said Tuensang District comprising elected representatives from the tribes therein. This Regional Council will supervise and guide the working of the village, Range and Area Council in that district and further no law passed by the Nagaland Legislature will extend to that district unless so recommended by Regional Council;

(i) religious or social practices of the Nagas;

(ii) Naga Customary Law and Procedure;

(iii) administration of civil and criminal justice involving decisions according to Naga Customary Law;

(iv) ownership and transfer of land and its resources.

As these matters are peculiar to the proposed new State of Nagaland provision with respect thereto has to be made in the Constitution itself. A separate Act, viz. the State of Nagaland Act, 1962, for the formation of the new State relatable to Art. 3 was also simultaneously passed.

(f) notwithstanding anything in the foregoing provisions of this clause, the final decision on all matters relating to the Tuensang district shall be made by the Governor in his discretion;

(g) in article 54, 55 and clause (4) of article 80, reference to the elected members of the Legislative Assembly of a State or to each such member shall include reference to the members or member of the Legislative Assembly of Nagaland elected by the Regional Council established under this article;

(h) in article 170 –

(i) clause (1) shall, in relation to the Legislative Assembly of Nagaland, have effect as if for the word 'sixty', the words 'forty-six' has been substituted;

(ii) in the said clause, the reference to direct election from territorial constituencies in the State shall include election by the members of the regional council established under this article;

(iii) in clauses (2) and (3), references to territorial constituencies shall mean references to territorial constituencies in the Kohima and Mokokchung districts.

3. If any difficulty arises in giving effect to any of the foregoing provisions of this article, the President may by order do anything (including any adoption or modification of any other article) which appears to him to be necessary for the purpose of the removing that difficulty;

Provided that no such order shall be made after the expiration of three years from the date of the formation of the State of Nagaland.

Explanation: In this article, the Kohima, Mokokchung and Tuensang districts shall have the same meanings as in the State of Nagaland Act, 1962.

Special Provisions with respect to the State of Assam

371B Notwithstanding anything in this Constitution, the President may, by order made with respect to the State of Assam, provide for the Constitution and functions of a committee of the Legislative Assembly of the State consisting of members of that Assembly elected from the tribal areas specified in Part-I[@] of table appended to paragraph 20 of the Sixth Schedule and such number of other members of that Assembly as may be specified in the order and for the modifications to be made in the rules of procedure of that Assembly for the constitution and proper functioning of such committee.

Special Provision with respect to the State of Manipur

371C*(1) Notwithstanding anything in this constitution, the President may, by order made with respect to the State of Manipur, provide for the Constitution, and functions of a Committee of the Legislative Assembly of the State consisting of members of that Assembly elected from the Hill Areas of that State, for the modifications to be made in the rules of business of the Government and in the rules of procedure of the Legislative Assembly of the State and for any special responsibility of the Governor in order to secure the proper functioning of such committee.

(2) The Governor shall annually, or whenever so required by the President, make a report to the President regarding the

---

Scope of Art. 371B – Article 371B was inserted by the Constitution (22nd Amendment) Act, 1969, w.e.f. 25.9.1969 in order to facilitate the creation of the sub-state 'Meghalaya'. Subsequently, by the North-Eastern Areas (Reorganisation) Act, 1971, Meghalaya has been admitted as a full-fledged State under Sch. I, post.

@ The figure 'I' was substituted for the letter 'A' by the N.E. Areas (Reorganisation) Act, 1971.

* Inserted by the Constitution (Twenty Seventh Amendment) Act, 1971.

administration of the Hill Areas in the State of Manipur and the executive power of the Union shall extend to the giving of directions to the State as to the administration of the said areas.

Explanation–In this article, the expression "Hill Areas" means such areas as the President may, by order, declare to be Hill Areas.

[371G Special provision with respect to the State of Mizoram – Notwithstanding anything in this Constitution,–

(a) No Act of Parliament in respect of–
  (i) religious or social practices of the Mizos,
  (ii) Mizo customary law and procedure,
  (iii) administration of civil and criminal justice involving decisions according to Mizo customary law,
  (iv) ownership and transfer of land,

shall apply to the State of Mizoram unless the Legislative Assembly of the State of Mizoram by a resolution so decides:

Provided that nothing in this clause shall apply to any Central Act in force in the Union territory of Mizoram immediately before the commencement of the Constitution (Fifty-third Amendment) Act, 1986;

(b) the Legislative Assembly of the State of Mizoram shall consist of not less than forty members.]

[371H Special provision with respect to the State of Arunachal Pradesh – Notwithstanding anything in this Constitution–

(a) the Governor of Arunachal Pradesh shall have special responsibility with respect to law and order in the state of Arunachal Pradesh and in the discharge of his functions in relation thereto, the Governor shall, after consulting the

Council of Ministers, exercise his individual judgement as to the action to be taken:

Provided that if any question arises whether any matter is or is not a matter as respects which the Governor is under this clause required to act in the exercise of his individual judgement, the decision of the Governor in his discretion shall be final, and the validity of any done by the Governor shall not be called in question on the ground that he ought or ought not to have acted in the exercise of his individual judgement:

Provided further that if the President on receipt of a report from the Governor or otherwise is satisfied that it is no longer necessary for the Governor to have special responsibility with respect to law and order in the State of Arunachal Pradesh, he may by order direct that the Governor shall cease to have such responsibility with effect from such date as may be specified in the order;

(b) the Legislative Assembly of the State of Arunachal Pradesh shall consist of not less than thirty members.]

2

Fifth Schedule to the Constitution specifying Scheduled Areas

[Article 244 (1)]

PROVISIONS AS TO THE ADMINISTRATION AND CONTROL OF SCHEDULED AREAS AND SCHEDULED TRIBES

PART A

GENERAL

Interpretation

1. In this Schedule, unless the context otherwise requires, the expression "State"... does not include the States of Assam, Meghalaya, Tripura and Mizoram.

Administration of Scheduled Areas and Tribes (Other than in Assam, Meghalaya, Tripura and Mizoram: While the Sixth Schedule deals with the administration of the Tribal Areas in Assam, Meghalaya, Tripura and Mizoram, the Fifth Schedule deals with the administration of other Scheduled Areas and Tribes (as enumerated under para 6 of the 5th Sch.)

The Fifth Schedule generally corresponds to the 'Excluded Areas and Partially Excluded Areas'. as referred to in Section 91 and 92 of the Government of India Act, 1935 and the Government of India (Excluded and Partially Excluded Areas). Order, 1936 (minus the Areas of Assam, which are included in the 6th Sch.)

The areas placed in the category of "Excluded Areas" were based upon strict necessity and limited in scope consistently with the needs of the tribal population. In regard to the areas classified as "Partially-Excluded" were areas containing a preponderance of the tribals which was of sufficient size to make possible the application of special legislation and special administration treatment. The inhabitants of these areas were not politically advanced. They required security of land tenure, protection for economic subjugation by their neighbours. freedom in the

(*Contd.*)

Executive Power of a State in Scheduled Areas

2. Subject to the provisions of this Schedule, the executive power of a State extends to the Scheduled areas therein.

Report by the Governor to President regarding the Administration of Scheduled Areas

3. The Governor of each State having Scheduled Areas therein shall annually, or whenever so required by the President, make a report to the President regarding the administration of the Scheduled Areas in that State and the executive power of the Union shall extend to the giving of directions to the State as to the administration of the said area.

---

pursuit of their traditional methods of livelihood and the reasonable exercises of their ancestral customs and manage their own affairs without any interference from outside. Keeping there principles in view, the Government of India declared the frontier and border regions in Assam, the Lakshadweep and Minicoy Island, the Lahaul and Spiti areas in Punjab as "Excluded Areas" and extensive tribal tracts in the Provinces of Madras, Bombay, Bengal, United Provinces, Bihar, Central Provinces and Orissa as "Partially-Excluded Areas".

The Scheduled Areas are determined by the President by an Order and such Order may be amended by the President from time to time except that he cannot alter an Order made under sub-paragraph 1 of para 6 except as laid down in Cls. (a), (b) and (c) of second sub-paragraph.

Any amendment of the Schedule must be made by Parliament.
The Schedule Tribes are enumerated by the Order of the President made under Art. 342, such as the Constitution (Scheduled Tribes) Order, 1950.

The executive power of the Union is to give directives to the State regarding the administration of the Scheduled Areas. Tribes Advisory Councils are constituted to give advice on such matters as welfare and advancement of the Scheduled Tribes in the States as may be referred to them by the Governor. Governor of the States in which there are Scheduled Areas have to submit reports to the President regarding the administration of such areas, annually or whenever so required by the President.

The Governor is authorised to direct that any particular Act of Parliament or the Legislature of the State shall not apply to a Scheduled Area or shall apply, only subject to exceptions or modifications. The Governor is also authorised to make regulations to prohibit or restrict the transfer of land by, or among members of, the Scheduled Tribes, regulate the allotment of land, and regulate the business of money-lending. All such regulations by the Governor must have the assent of the President.

(Contd.)

PART B

Administration and Control of Scheduled Areas and Scheduled Tribes

4. Tribal Advisory Council — (1) There shall be established in each State having Scheduled Areas therein and, if the President so directs, also in any State having Scheduled Tribes but not Scheduled Areas therein , a Tribes Advisory Council consisting of not more than twenty members of whom, as nearly as may be, three-fourths shall be the representatives of the Scheduled Tribes in the Legislative Assembly of the State;

Provided that if the number of representatives of the Scheduled Tribes in the Legislative Assembly of the State is less than the number of seats in the Tribes Advisory Council to be filled by such representatives, the remaining seats shall be filled by other members of those tribes.

In short, the Governor is the sole legislature for the Scheduled Areas and Tribes to which this Schedule applies. He make Regulations after consulting the Tribes Advisory Council and submits them to the President for the latter's assent.

The Scheduled Areas have been constituted with two clear and straightforward objectives. One is to assist the tribals in enjoying their existing rights unhindered or unobstructed by others through summary processes. The second is to develop the Scheduled areas and promoted the economic, educational and social progress of the Scheduled Tribes.

Entries 19-22 were substituted by North-Eastern Areas (Reorganisation) Act, 1971.

Inserted by the Constitution (36th Amendment) Act, 1975.

Scheduled Areas are in the States of Andhra Pradesh, Bihar, Gujarat, Himachal Pradesh, Madhya Pradesh, Maharashtra, Orissa and Rajasthan.

The Act of Parliament or of the appropriate Legislature apply to the Scheduled Areas of their own force, but the Governor has the power to exclude their operation by a notification. In the absence of such a notification, therefore, the Acts of the Legislature shall extend to such areas.

The power of making a notification under the present Clause is legislative power, and, in making a notification, the Governor is competent to change the whole aspect of an Act or Section referred to in the notification.

(2) It shall be the duty of the Tribes Advisory Council to advise on such matters pertaining to the welfare and advancement of the Scheduled Tribes in the State as may be referred to them by the Governor.

(3) The Governor may make rules prescribing or regulating as the case may be:

(a) The number of members of the Council, the mode of their appointment and the appointment of the Chairman of the Council and of the officers and servants thereof;
(b) The conduct of its meetings and its procedure in general; and
(c) All other incidental matters.

Law Applicable to Scheduled Areas

5. (1) Notwithstanding anything in this Constitution, the Governor may by public notification direct that any particular act of Parliament or of Legislature of the State shall not apply to a Scheduled Area or any part thereof in the State subject to such exceptions and modifications as he may specify in the notification and any direction given under this sub-paragraph may be given as to have retrospective effect.

(2) The Governor may make regulations for the peace and good government of any area in a State which is for the time being a Scheduled Area. In particular and without prejudice to the generality of the foregoing power, such regulations may–

(a) prohibit or restrict the transfer of land by or among members of the Scheduled Tribes in such area;
(b) regulate the allotment of land to members of the Scheduled Tribes in such area; and
(c) regulate the carrying on the business as money-lender by persons who lend money to members of the Scheduled Tribes in such area.

(3) In making any such regulation as is referred to in sub-paragraph (2) of this paragraph, the Governor may repeal or amend any act of Parliament or of Legislature of the State or any existing law which is for the time being applicable to the area in question.

(4) All regulations made under this paragraph shall be submitted forthwith to the President and, until assented to by him, shall have no effect.

(5) No regulation shall be made under this paragraph unless the Governor making the regulation has, in the case where there is a Tribes Advisory Council for the State, consulted such council.

PART C

SCHEDULED AREAS

6. **Scheduled Areas** – (1) In this Constitution, the expression "Scheduled Areas" means such areas as the President may by order declare to be Scheduled Areas.

(2) The President may at any time by order:

(a) direct that the whole or any specified part of a Scheduled Area shall cease to be a Scheduled Area or a part of such an area;

(aa) increase the area of any Scheduled Area in a State after consultation with the Governor of that State;

(b) alter, but only by way of rectification of boundaries, any Scheduled Area;

(c) on any alteration of the boundaries of a State or on the admission into the union or the establishment of a new State, declare any territory not previously included in any State to be, or to form part of, a Scheduled Area;

(d)* rescind in relation to any State or States, any order or orders made under this paragraph, and in consultation with the Governor of the State concerned, make fresh order redefining the areas which are to be Scheduled Areas; and, any such order may contain such incidental and consequential provisions as appear to the President to be necessary and proper, but save as aforesaid, the order made under sub-paragraph (1) of this paragraph shall not be varied by any subsequent order.

PART D

AMENDMENT OF THE SCHEDULE

7. **Amendment of the Schedule** – (1) Parliament may from time to time by law amend by way of addition, variation or repeal any or the provisions of this Schedule and, when the Schedule is so amended, any reference to this Schedule in this Constitution shall be construed as a reference to such Schedule as so amended.

(2) No such law as is mentioned in sub-paragraph (1) of this paragraph shall be deemed to be an amendment of this Constitution for the purposes of article 368.

---

* Inserted by the Constitution (42nd Amendment) Act 1976 w.e.f. 7.9.1976. While some progress has been made in the functioning of the Fifth Schedule, it has been found that the object with which the Scheduled Areas were formed has been realised only partially. The Governors are not playing their roles effectively.

3

Sixth Schedule to the Constitution regarding Administration of Tribal Areas in the States of Assam, Meghalaya, Tripura and Mizoram*

[Articles 244 (2) and 275(1)]

PROVISIONS AS TO THE ADMINISTRATION OF TRIBAL AREAS IN THE STATES OF ASSAM, MEGHALAYA, TRIPURA[1] AND MIZORAM[1]

1. Autonomous Districts and Autonomous Regions

(1) Subject to the provisions of this paragraph, the tribal areas

---

Extensive changes have been made in the Sixth Schedule by the North-Eastern Areas (Reorganisation) Act, 1971, the Constitution (49th Amendment) Act, 1984 and the Sixth Schedule to the Constitution (Amendment) Act, 1988. The Table in para 20 has been recast into Parts I, II, IIA, and III (instead of A and B) and all the four Parts have been constituted autonomous districts, to be governed by the same provisions. The four Parts indicate that the territories appertain to the States of Assam, Meghalaya, Tripura and Mizoram, respectively

Administration of Tribal Areas in Assam, Meghalaya, Tripura and Mizoram. As amended by the above Acts, there are four Parts in the Table appended to the Schedule. Each of these Areas shall be an 'autonomous district' by virtue of the Constitution, and the provisions in paras 1-17 relate to the Administration of these Autonomous districts, the word 'autonomous' indicating a right of self-government.

These are divided in Parts I, II, IIA, and III in order to distinguish that the Areas in Part I represent the Tribal Areas of Assam, while Part II includes the Tribal Areas of Meghalaya, Part-IIA pertains to Tripura and Part III represents Tribal Areas in Mizoram.

* The Sixth Schedule in its application to Assam has been modified by Act 42 of 1995. For the text of the Act, see Appendix II.

1. Substituted by the Constitution (49th Amendment) Act, 1984.

in each item of Parts I, II and IIA, and Part III of the table appended to paragraph 20 of this Schedule shall be an autonomous district.

(2) If there are different Scheduled Tribes in an autonomous district, Governor may, by the public notification, divide the area or areas inhabited by them into autonomous regions.

(3) The Governor may, by public notification:

(a) include any area in any of the parts of the said table;
(b) exclude any area from any of the parts of the said table;
(c) create a new autonomous district;
(d) increase the area of any autonomous district;
(e) diminish the area of any autonomous district;
(f) unite two or more autonomous districts or parts thereof as to form one autonomous district.
(ff) alter the name of any autonomous district; and
(g) define the boundaries of any autonomous district:

Provided that no order shall be made by the Governor under clauses (c), (d), (e) and (f) of this sub-paragraph except after consideration of the report of a Commission appointed under sub-paragraph (1) of the paragraph 14 of this Schedule.

Provided further that any order made by the Governor under this sub-paragraph may contain such incidental and consequential provisions (including any amendment of paragraph 20 and of any item in any of the Parts of the said table) as appear to the Governor to be necessary for giving effect to the provisions of the order.

2. Constitution of District Councils and Regional Councils

(1) There shall be a District Council for each autonomous district consisting of not more than thirty members, of whom not more than four persons shall be nominated by the Governor and the rest shall be elected on the basis of adult suffrage.

(2) There shall be a separate Regional Council for each area constituted an autonomous region under sub-paragraph (2) of paragraph 1 of this Schedule.

(3) Each District Council and each Regional Council shall be a body corporate by the name respectively of "the District Council of (name of district)" and "the Regional Council of (name of region)", shall have perpetual succession and a common seal and shall by the said name sue and be sued.

(4) Subject to the provisions of this Schedule, the administration of an autonomous district shall in so far as it is not vested under this Schedule in any Regional Council within such district, be vested in the District Council for such district and the administration of an autonomous region shall be vested in the Regional Council for such region.[@]

(5) In an autonomous district with Regional Councils, the District Council shall have only such powers with respect to the areas under the authority of the Regional Council may be delegated to it by the Regional Council in addition to the powers conferred on it by this Schedule with respect to such areas.

(6) The Governor shall make rules for the first Constitution of District Councils and Regional Councils[X] in consultation with the existing Tribal Councils or other representative tribal organisations within the autonomous districts or regions concerned and such rules shall provide for:

(a) the composition of the District Councils and Regional Councils and the allocation of seats therein;

(b) the delimitation of territorial constituencies for the purpose of elections to those Councils;

(c) the qualifications for voting at such elections and the preparation of electoral rolls therefor;

@ The second Proviso was added by the North-Eastern Area (Reorganisation) Act, 1971.

X Substituted by the Assam Reorganisation (Meghalaya) Act, 1969.

(d) the qualifications for being elected at such elections as members of such Councils;

(e) the term of office of members of Regional Councils;

(f) any other matter relating to or connected with elections or nominations to such Councils;

(g) the procedure and the conduct of business including the power to act notwithstanding any vacancy in the District and Regional Councils; and

(h) the appointment of officers and staff of the District and the Regional Councils.

6A* The elected members of the District Councils shall hold office for a term of five years from the date appointed for the first meeting of the Council after the general elections to the Council, unless the District Council is sooner dissolved under paragraph 16 and a nominated member shall hold office at the pleasure of the Governor.

Provided that the said period of five years may, while a Proclamation of Emergency is in operation or if circumstances exist, which, in the opinion of the Governor, render the holding of elections impracticable, be extended by the Governor for a period not exceeding one year at a time and in any case where a Proclamation of Emergency is in operation not extending beyond a period of six months after the Proclamation has ceased to operate.

Provided further that a member elected to fill a casual vacancy shall hold office only for the remainder of the term of office of the member whom he replaces.

---

* Changes made by the Assam Reorganisation (Meghalaya) Act, 1969 (w.e.f. 2.4.70).

The second proviso has been omitted by the Assam Reorganisation (Meghalaya) Act, 1969.

7. The District or the Regional Council may alter its first Constitution make rules with the approval of the Governor with regard to the matters specified in sub-paragraph (6) of this paragraph and may also make rules with like approval regulating–

(a) the formation of subordinate local Councils of Boards and their procedure and the conduct of their business; and
(b) generally all matters relating to the transaction of business pertaining to the administration of the District or region, as the case may be:

Provided that until rules are made by the District or the Regional Council under this sub-paragraph the rules made by the Governor under sub-paragraph (6) of this paragraph shall have effect in respect of elections to, the officers and staff of, and the procedure and the conduct of business in, such Council.

3. Powers of the District Council and Regional Councils to make laws

(1) The Regional Council for an autonomous region in respect of all areas within such region and the District Council for an autonomous district in respect of all areas within the district except those which are under the authority of Regional Councils, if any, within the district shall have power to make laws with respect to –

(a) The allotment, occupation or use, or the setting apart, of land, other than any land which is reserved forest, for the purposes of agriculture or grazing or for residential or other non-agricultural purposes or for any other purpose likely to promote the interests for the inhabitants of any village or town:

Provided that nothing in such laws shall prevent the compulsory acquisition of any land, whether occupied or unoccupied, for public purposes by the Government of the State concerned* in accordance with the law for the time being in force authorising such acquisition.

(b) the management of any forest not being a reserved forest;
(c) the use of any canal or water-course for the purpose of agriculture;
(d) the regulation of the practice of jhum or other forms of shifting cultivation;
(e) the establishment of village or town committees or councils and their powers;
(f) any other matter relating to village or town administration, including village or town police and public health and sanitation;
(g) the appointment or succession of Chiefs or headmen;
(h) the inheritance of property;
(i) marriage and divorce; and
(j) social customs.

(2) In this paragraph a "reserved forest" means any area which is a reserved forest under the Assam Forest Regulation, 1891, or under any other law for the time being in force in the area in question.

(3) All laws made under this paragraph shall be submitted forthwith to the Governor and, until assented by him, shall have no effect.

4. Administration of Justice in Autonomous Districts and Autonomous Regions

(1) The Regional Council for an autonomous region in respect of areas within such region and the District Councils for an autonomous district in respect of areas within the

* Substituted by the North-Eastern Areas (Reorganisation) Act, 1971.

district other than those which are under the authority of the Regional Councils, if any, within the district may constitute village councils or courts for the trial of suits and cases between the parties all of whom belong to the Scheduled Tribes within such areas, other than suits and cases to which the provisions of sub-paragraph (1) of paragraph 5 of this Schedule apply, to the exclusion of any court in the State, and may appoint suitable persons to be members of such village councils or presiding officers of such courts and may also appoint such officers as may be necessary for the administration of the laws made under paragraph 3 of this Schedule.

(2) Notwithstanding anything in this Constitution, the Regional Council for an autonomous region or any court constituted in that behalf by the Regional Council or, if in respect of an area within an autonomous district there is no Regional Council, the district Council for such district or any court constituted in that behalf by the District Council, shall exercise the powers of a court of appeal in respect of all suits and cases triable by a village area, as the case may be, other than those to which the provisions of sub-paragraph (1) of paragraph 5 of this Schedule apply, and no other court except the High Court and the Supreme Court shall have jurisdiction over such suits or cases.

(3) The High Court...shall have and exercise such jurisdiction over the suits and cases to which the provisions of sub-paragraph (2) of this paragraph apply as the Governor may from time to time order specify.

(4) A Regional Council or District Council, as the case may be, may with the previous approval of the Governor makes rules regulating –

(a) the Constitution of village councils and courts and the powers to be exercised by them under this paragraph;

(b) the procedure to be followed by village councils or courts in the trial of suits and cases under sub-paragraph (1) of this paragraph;

(c) the procedure to be followed by the Regional or District Council or any court constituted by such Council in appeals and other proceedings under sub-paragraph (2) of this paragraph;

(d) the enforcement of decisions and order of such councils and courts; and

(e) all other ancillary matters for the carrying out of the provisions of sub-paragraph (1) and (2) of this paragraph.

(5) On and from such date as the President may, after consulting the Government of the State concerned, by notification appoint in this behalf, this paragraph shall have effect in relation to such autonomous district or region as may be specified in the notification, as if –

(i) In sub-paragraph (1) for the words "between the parties all of whom belong to Scheduled Tribes within such areas, other than suits and cases to which the provisions of sub-paragraph (1) of paragraph 5 of this Schedule apply" the words "not being suits and cases of the nature referred to in sub-paragraph (1) of paragraph 5 of this Schedule, which the Governor may specify in this behalf", had been substituted;

(ii) in the sub-paragraphs (2) and (3) had been omitted;

(iii) in sub-paragraph (4) –

(a) for the words "A Regional Council or District Council, as the case may be, may with the previous approval of the Governor make rules regulating", the words "The Governor may make rules regulating" had been substituted; and

(b) for clause (a), the following clause had been substituted, namely:-

"(a) the constitution of village councils and courts, the powers to be exercised by them under this paragraph and the courts shall lie".

(c) for clause (c), the following clause had been substituted, namely:

"(c) the transfer of appeals and other proceedings pending before the Regional or District Council or any court constituted by such Council immediately before the date appointed by the President under sub-paragraph (5)"; and

(d) in clause (e), for the words, bracket and figures "subparagraph (1) and (2)", the word brackets and figure "sub-paragraph (1)" had been substituted.

5. Conferment of powers under the Code of Civil Procedure, 1908, and the Code of Criminal Procedure, 1898 on the Regional and District Councils and on Certain Courts and Officers for the Trial of Certain Suits, Cases and Offences

(1) The Governors may, for the trial of suits or cases arising out of any law in force in any autonomous district or region being a law specified in that behalf by the Governor, or for the trial of offences punishable with death, transportation for life, or imprisonment for a term of not less than five years under the Indian Penal Code or under any other law for the time being applicable to such district or region, confer on the District Council or the Regional Council having authority over such district or region or on courts constituted by such District Council or on any officer appointed in that behalf by the Governor, such powers under the Code of Civil Procedure, 1908, or as the case may be, the Code of Criminal Procedure, 1898, as he deems appropriate and thereupon the said council, court or officer shall try the suits, cases or offences in exercise of the powers so conferred.

(2) The Governor may withdraw or modify any of the powers conferred on a District Council, Regional Council, Court or officer under sub-paragraph (1) of this paragraph.

(3) Save as expressly provided in this paragraph, the Code of Civil Procedure, 1908 and the Code of Criminal

Procedure, 1898, shall not apply to the trial of any suits, cases or offences in an autonomous district or in any autonomous region to which the provisions of this paragraph apply.

(4) On and from the date appointed by the President under sub-paragraph (5) of paragraph 4 in relation to any autonomous district or autonomous region, nothing contained in this paragraph shall, in its application to that district or region, be deemed to authorise the Governor to confer on the District Council or Regional Council or on courts constituted by the District Council any of the powers referred to in sub-paragraph (1) of this paragraph.

6. Powers of the District Council to establish Primary Schools, etc.

(1) The District Council for an autonomous district may establish, construct, or manage primary schools, dispensaries, cattle pounds, ferries, fisheries, roads, road transport and waterways in the district and may, with the previous approval of the Governor, make regulations for the regulation and control thereof and, in particular, may prescribe the language and the manner in which primary education shall be imparted in the primary schools in the district.

(2) The Governor may, with the consent of any District Council entrust either conditionally or unconditionally to that Council or its officers functions in relation to agriculture, animal husbandry, communities projects, co-operative societies, social welfare, village planning or any other matter to which the executive power of the State extends.

7. District and Regional Funds

(1) There shall be constituted for each autonomous district, a District Fund for each autonomous region, a Regional Fund

to which shall be credited all moneys received respectively by the District Council for that district and the Regional Council for that region in the course of the administration of such district or region, as the case may be, in accordance with the provisions of this Constitution.

(2) The Governor may make rules for the management of the District Fund, or, as the case may be, the Regional Fund, and for the procedure to be followed in respect of payment of money into the said fund, the withdrawal of moneys therefrom, the custody of moneys therein and any other matter connected with or ancillary to the matters aforesaid.

(3) The accounts of the District Council or, as the case may be, the Regional Council shall be kept in such form as the Comptroller and Auditor-General of India may, with the approval of the President, prescribe.

(4) The Comptroller and Auditor-General shall cause the accounts of the District and Regional Councils to be audited in such manner as he may thing fit, and the reports of the Comptroller and Auditor-General relating to such accounts shall be submitted to the Governor who shall cause them to be laid before the Council.

8. Powers to Assess and Collect Land Revenue and to Impose Taxes

(1) The Regional Council for an autonomous region in respect of all lands within such region and the District Council for an autonomous district in respect of all lands within the district except those which are in the areas under the authority of Regional Councils, if any, within the district, shall have the power to assess and collect revenue in respect of such lands in accordance with the principles for the time being followed by the Government of the State in assessing lands for the purpose of land revenue in the state generally.

(2) The Regional Council for autonomous region in respect of areas within such region and the District Council for autonomous district in respect of all areas in the district except those which are under the authority of Regional Councils, if any, within the district, shall have power to levy and collect taxes on lands and buildings, and tolls on persons resident within such areas.

(3) The District Council for an autonomous district shall have the power to levy and collect all or any of the following taxes within such district, that is to say –

(a) Taxes on professions, trades callings and employments;

(b) Taxes on animals, vehicles and boats;

(c) Taxes on the entry of goods into a market for sale therein, and tolls on passengers and goods carried in ferries; and

(d) Taxes for the maintenance of schools, dispensaries or roads.

(4) A Regional Council or District Council, as the case may be, may make regulations to provide for the levy and collection any of the taxes specified in sub-paragraphs (2) and (3) of this paragraph and every such regulations shall be submitted forthwith to the Governor and, until assented to by him, shall have no effect.

9. Licences or Leases for the Purposes of Prospecting for, or Extracting of, Minerals

(1) Such share of the royalties accruing each year from licences or leases for the purpose of prospective for, or the extraction of, minerals granted by the Government of the State in respect of any area within an autonomous district as may be agreed upon between the Government of the State and the District Council of such district shall be made over to that District Council.

(2) If any dispute arises as to the share of such royalties to be made over to a District Council, it shall be referred to the Governor for determination and the amount determined by the Governor in discretion shall be deemed to be the amount payable under sub-paragraph (1) of this paragraph to the District Council and the decision of the Governor shall be final.

(3)* The Governor may, by order, direct that the share of royalties to be made over to a District council under this paragraph shall be made over to that Council within a period of one year from the date of any agreement under sub-paragraph (1) or, as the case may be, of any determination under sub-paragraph (2).

10. Powers of District Councils to make regulations for the control of money-lending and trading

(1) This District Council of an autonomous district may make regulations for the regulation and control of money-lending or trading within the district by persons* resident in the district.

(2) In particular and without prejudice to the generality of the foregoing power, such regulations may –

(a) prescribe that no one except the holder of a licence issued in that behalf shall carry on the business of money-lending;

(b) prescribe the maximum rate of interest which may be charged or be recovered by a money-lender;

(c) provide for the maintenance of accounts by money-lenders and for the inspection of such accounts by officers appointed in that behalf by the District Council;

(d) prescribe that no person resident in the district shall carry on any trade, whether wholesale or retail, except under a licence issued in that behalf by the District Council.

---

* Inserted by the 6th Sch. to the Constitution (Amendment) Act 67 of 1988 in its application to the States of Tripura and Mizoram.

Provided that no regulations may be made under this paragraph unless they are passed by a majority of not less than three-fourths of the total memberships of the District Council.

Provided further that it shall not be competent under any such regulations to refuse the grant of a licence to a money-lender or a trader who has been carrying on business within the district since before the time of the making of such regulations.

(3) All regulations made under this paragraph shall be submitted forthwith to the Governor and, until assented to by him, shall have no effect.

11. Publication of Laws, Rules and Regulations made under the Schedule

All laws, rules and regulations made under this Schedule by a District Council or a Regional Council shall be published forthwith in the official gazette of the State and shall on such publication have the force of law.

12. Application of Acts of Parliament and of the Legislature of the State of Assam to Autonomous Districts and Autonomous Regions in the State of Assam

(1) Notwithstanding anything in this Constitution,–

(a) No act of the Legislature of the State of Assam in respect of any of the matters specified in paragraph 3 of this Schedule as matters with respect to which a District Council or a Regional Council may make laws, and no act of the Legislature of the State of Assam prohibiting or restricting the consumption of any non-distilled alcoholic liquor shall apply to any autonomous district or autonomous region is that State unless in either case the District Council for such district or having jurisdiction over such region by public notification so directs, and the District Council in giving such direction with respect to any Act may direct that the Act shall in its application to such district or region or any part thereof have effect subject to such exceptions or modifications as it thinks fit;

(b) The Governor may, by public notification, direct that any Act of Parliament or of the Legislature of the State of Assam of which the provisions of clause (a) of this sub-paragraph do not apply, shall not apply to an autonomous district or an autonomous region in that State or shall apply to such district or region or any part thereof subject to such exceptions or modifications as he may specify in the notification.

(2) Any direction given under sub-paragraph (1) of this paragraph may be given so as to have retrospective effect.

12A. Application of Acts of Parliament and of the Legislature of State of Meghalaya to autonomous districts and autonomous regions in the State of Meghalaya

Notwithstanding anything in this Constitution,—

(a) if any provision of a law made by a District or Regional Council in the State of Meghalaya with respect to any matter specified in sub-paragraph (1) of paragraph 3 of this Schedule or if any provision of any regulation made by a District Council or a Regional Council in that State under paragraph 8 or paragraph 10 of this Schedule, is repugnant to any provision of a law made by the Legislature of the State of Meghalaya with respect to that matter, then, the law or regulation made by the District Council or, as the case may be, the Regional Council, whether made before or after the law made by the Legislature of the State of Meghalaya, shall, to the extent of repugnancy, be void and the law made by the Legislature of the State of Meghalaya shall prevail;

(b) the President may, with respect to any Act of Parliament, by notification, direct that it shall not apply to an autonomous district or an autonomous region in the State of Meghalaya, or shall apply to such district or region or any other part thereof subject to such exceptions or modifications as he may specify in the notification and any such direction may be given so as to have retrospective effect.

12AA. Application of Acts of Parliament and the Legislature of the State of Tripura to the autonomous district and autonomous regions in the State of Tripura

Notwithstanding anything in the Constitution,—

(a) no Act of the Legislature of the State of Tripura in respect of any of the matters specified in paragraph 3 of this Schedule as matters with respect to which a District Council or a Regional Council may make laws, and no Act of the Legislature of the State of Tripura prohibiting or restricting the consumption of any non-distilled alcoholic liquor shall apply to the autonomous district or an autonomous region in that State unless, in either case, the District Council for that District or having jurisdiction over such region by public notification so directs, and the District Council in giving such direction with respect to any Act may direct that the Act shall, in its application to that district or such region or any part thereof, have effect subject to such exceptions or modifications as it thinks fit;

AA This paragraph was first inserted by the Constitution (49th Amendment) Act, 1984 and then substituted by the 6th Sch. to the Constitution (Amendment) Act 67 of 1988, in its application to the States of Tripura and Mizoram.

(b) the Governor may, by public notification, direct that any Act of the Legislature of the State of Tripura to which the provisions of clause (a) of this sub-paragraph do not apply, shall not apply to the autonomous district or an autonomous region in that State, or shall apply to that district or such region, or any part thereof, subject to such exceptions or modifications, as he may specify in the notification;

(c) the President may with respect to any Act of Parliament, by notification, direct that it shall not apply to the autonomous district or an autonomous region in the State of Tripura, or shall apply to such district or region or any part thereof, subject to such exceptions or modifications as he may specify in the notification and any such direction may be given so as to have retrospective effect.

12B. Application of Acts of Parliament and of the Legislature of the State of Mizoram to autonomous districts and autonomous regions in the State of Mizoram

Notwithstanding anything in this Constitution,–

(a) no Act of the Legislature of the State of Mizoram in respect of any of the matters specified in paragraph 3 of this Schedule as matters with respect to which a District Council or a Regional Council may make laws, and no Act of the Legislature of the State of Mizoram prohibiting or restricting the consumption of any non-distilled alcoholic liquor shall apply to the autonomous district or an autonomous region in that State unless, in either case, the District Council for such District or having jurisdiction over such region by public notification, so directs, and the District Council, in giving such direction with respect to any Act, may direct that the Act shall, in its application to such district or region or any part thereof, have effect subject to such exceptions or modifications as it thinks fit;

(b) the Governor may, by public notification, direct that any Act of the Legislature of the State of Mizoram to which the provisions of clause (a) of this sub-paragraph do not apply, shall not apply the autonomous district or an autonomous region in that State, or shall apply to such district or region, or any part thereof, subject to such exceptions or modifications, as he may specify in the notification;

(c) the President may with respect to any Act of Parliament, by notification, direct that it shall not apply to the autonomous district or an autonomous region in the State of Mizoram, or shall apply to such district or region or any part thereof, subject to such exceptions or modifications as he may specify in the notification and any such direction may be given so as to have retrospective effect.

13. Estimated receipts and expenditure pertaining to Autonomous Districts to be shown Separately in the Annual Financial Statement

The estimated receipts and expenditure pertaining to an autonomous district which are to be credited to, or is to be made from, the Consolidated Fund of the State shall be first placed before the District Council for discussion and then after such discussion be shown separately in the Annual Financial Statement of the State to be laid before the Legislature of the State under article 202.

14. Appointment of Commission to inquire into and Report on the Administration of Autonomous Districts and Autonomous Regions

(1) The Governor may at any time appoint a Commission to examine and report on any matter specified by him relating

to the administration of the autonomous districts and autonomous regions in the State, including matters specified in clauses (c), (d), (e) and (f) of sub-paragraph (3) of paragraph 1 of this Schedule, or may appoint a Commission to inquire into and report from time to time on the administration of autonomous district and autonomous regions in the State generally and in particular on —

(a) the provision of education and medical facilities and communications in such districts and regions;
(b) the need for any new or special legislation in respect of such districts and regions; and
(c) the administration of the laws, rules and regulations made by the District and Regional Councils;

and define the procedure to be followed by such Commission.

(2) The report of every such Commission with the recommendations of the Governor with respect thereto shall be laid before the Legislature of the State by the Minister concerned together with an explanatory memorandum regarding the action proposed to be taken thereon by the Government of the State.

(3) In allocating the business of the Government of the State among his Ministers the Governor may place one of his Ministers specially in charge of the welfare of the autonomous regions in the State.

15. Annulment or Suspension of Acts and Resolutions of District and Regional Councils

(1) If at any time the Governor is satisfied that an act or resolution of a District or a Regional Council is likely to endanger the safety of India or is likely to be prejudicial to public order, he may annul or suspend such act or resolution and take such steps as he may consider necessary (including the

suspension of the Council and the assumption to himself of all or any of the powers vested in or exercisable by the Council) to prevent the Commission or continuance of such act, or the giving of effect to such resolution.

(2) Any order made by the Governor under sub-paragraph (1) of this paragraph together with the reasons therefor shall be laid before the Legislature of the State as soon as possible and the order shall, unless revoked by him continue in force for a period of twelve months from the date on which it was so made.

Provided that if and so often as a resolution approving the continuance in force of such order is passed by the Legislature of the State, the order shall unless cancelled by the Governor continue in force for a further period of twelve months from the date on which under this paragraph it would otherwise have ceased to operate.

16. Dissolution of a District or a Regional Council

(1) The Governor may on the recommendation of a Commission appointed under paragraph 14 of this Schedule by Public Notification order the dissolution of a District or a Regional Council, and—

(a) direct that a fresh general election shall be held immediately for the reconstitution of the Council, or

(b) assume the administration of the area under the authority of such Council himself or place the administration of such area under the Commission appointed under the said paragraph or any other body considered suitable by him for a period not exceeding twelve months:

Provided that when an order under clause (a) of this paragraph has been made, the Governor may take the action referred to in clause (b) of this paragraph with regard to the administration of the area in question pending the reconstitution of the Council on fresh general election.

Provided further that no action shall be taken under clause (b) of this paragraph without giving the District or the Regional Council, as the case may be, an opportunity of placing its views before the Legislature of the State.

(2) If at any time the Governor is satisfied that a situation has arisen in which the administration of an autonomous district or region cannot be carried on in accordance with the provisions of this Schedule, he may, by public notification, assume to himself all or any of the functions or powers vested in or exercisable by the District Council or, as the case may be, the Regional Council and declare that such functions or powers shall be exercisable by such person or authority as he may specify in this behalf, for a period not exceeding six months.

Provided that the Governor may by a further order or orders extend the operation of initial order by a period not exceeding six months on each occasion.

(3) Every order made under sub-paragraph (1) or sub-paragraph (2) of this paragraph, alongwith the reasons therefor shall be laid before the Legislature of the State.

17. Exclusion of areas from Autonomous Districts in forming Constituencies in such districts

For the purposes of elections to the Legislative Assembly of Assam or Meghalaya or Tripura or Mizoram, the Governor may by order declare that any area within an autonomous district in the State of Assam or Meghalaya or Tripura or Mizoram as the case may be, shall not form part of any constituency to fill a seat or seats in the Assembly reserved for any such district but shall form part of a constituency to fill a seat or seats in the Assembly not so reserved to be specified in the order.

18. Omitted by the North-Eastern Areas (Reorganisation) Act, 1971

19. Traditional Provisions

(1) As soon as possible after the commencement of this Constitution the Governor shall take steps for the constitution of a District Council for each autonomous district in the State under this Schedule and, until a District Council is so constituted for an autonomous district, the administration of such district shall be vested in the Governor and the following provisions shall apply to the administration of the areas within such district instead of the foregoing provisions of this Schedule, namely —

(a) no act of Parliament or of the Legislature of the State shall apply to any such area unless the Governor by public notification so directs; and the Governor in giving such a direction with respect to any Act may direct that the Act shall, in its application to the area or to any specified part thereof, have effect subject to such exceptions or modifications as he thinks fit;

(b) the Governor may make regulations for the peace and good government of any such area and any regulations so made may repeal or amend any Act of Parliament or of the Legislature of the State or any existing law which is for the time being applicable to such area.

(2) Any direction given by the Governor under clause (a) of sub-paragraph (1) of this paragraph may be given so as to have retrospective effect.

(3) All regulations made under clause (b) of sub-paragraph (1) of this paragraph shall be submitted forthwith to the President and, until assented to by him, shall have no effect.

20. Tribal Areas

(1) The areas specified in Parts I, II, IIA and III of the table below shall be the Tribal Areas within the State of Assam, the State of Meghalaya, the State of Tripura and the State of Mizoram.

(2) Any reference in Part I, Part II, Part III of the table below to any district shall be constructed as a reference to the territories comprised within the autonomous district of that name existing immediately before the day appointed under clause (b) of section 2 of the North-Eastern Areas (Reorganisation) Act, 1971:

Provided that for the purposes of clauses (e) and (f) of sub-paragraph (1) of paragraph 3, paragraph 4, paragraph 5, paragraph 6, sub-paragraph (2), clauses (a), (b) and (d) of sub-paragraph (3) and sub-paragraph (4) of paragraph 8 and clause (d) of sub-paragraph (3) of paragraph 10 of this Schedule, no part of the area comprised within the municipality of Shillong shall be deemed to be within the Khasi Hills District.

(3) The reference in Part IIA in the Table below to the "Tripura Tribal Areas District" shall be construed as a reference to the territory comprising the tribal areas specified in the First Schedule to the Tripura Tribal Areas Autonomous District Council, 1979.

TABLE

PART I

1. The North Cachar Hills District.
2. The Karbi Anglong District.

PART II

1. Khasi Hills District
2. Jaintia Hills District
3. The Garo Hills District

PART IIA

1. Tripura Tribal Areas District

PART III

(B)1. The Chakma District
2. The Mara District
3. The Lai District

20A. Dissolution of the Mizo District Council

(1) Notwithstanding anything in this Schedule, the District Council or the Mizo District existing immediately before the prescribed date (hereinafter referred to as the Mizo District Council) shall stand dissolved and cease to exist.

(2) The administrator of the Union territory of Mizoram may, by one or more orders, provide for all or any of the following matters, namely—

(a) the transfer, in whole or in part, of the assets, rights and liabilities of the Mizo District Council (including the rights and liabilities under any contract by it) to the Union or to any other authority;

(b) the substitution of the Union or any other authority for the Mizo District Council, or the addition of the Union or any other authority, as a party to any legal proceedings, to which the Mizo District Council is a party;

(c) the transfer or re-employment of any employees of the Mizo District Council to or by the Union or any other authority, the terms and conditions of service applicable to such employees after such transfer or re-employment;

(d) the continuance of any laws, made by the Mizo District Council and in force immediately before its dissolution, subject to such adaptations and modifications, whether by way of repeal or amendment, as the Administrator may make in this behalf, until such laws are altered, repealed or amended by a competent Legislature or other competent authority; and

(e) such incidental, consequential and supplementary matters as the Administrator considers necessary.

Explanation : In this paragraph and in paragraph 20B of this Schedule, the expression 'prescribed date' means the date on which the Legislative Assembly of the Union Territory of Mizoram is duly constituted under and in accordance with the provisions of the Government of Union Territories Act, 1963.

20B. Autonomous regions in the Union Territory of Mizoram to be Autonomous Districts and Transitory Provisions consequent thereto

(1) Notwithstanding anything in this Schedule,—

(a) every autonomous region existing immediately before the prescribed date in the Union territory of Mizoram shall, on and from that date, be an autonomous district in the Union territory (hereinafter referred to as the corresponding new district) and the Administrator thereof may, by one or more orders, direct that such consequential amendments as are necessary to give effect to the provisions of this clause shall be made in paragraph 20 of this Schedule (including Part III of the table appended to that paragraph) and thereupon the said paragraph and the said Part III shall be deemed to have been amended accordingly.

(b) Every Regional Council of an autonomous region in the Union territory of Mizoram existing immediately before the prescribed date (thereafter referred to as the existing Regional Council) shall, on and from that date and until a District Council of that district (hereafter referred to as the corresponding new District Council).

(2) Every member whether elected or nominated of an existing Regional Council shall be deemed to have been elected or, as the case may be, nominated to the corresponding new District Council and shall hold office until a District is duly constituted for the corresponding new district under this Schedule.

(3) Until rules are made under sub-paragraph (7) of paragraph 2 and sub-paragraph (4) of paragraph 4 of this Schedule by the corresponding new District Council, the rules made under the said provisions by the existing Regional Council and in force immediately before the prescribed date shall have effect in relation to the corresponding new District Council subject to such adaptations and modifications as may be made therein by the Administrator of the Union territory of Mizoram.

(4) The Administrator of the Union territory of Mizoram, may, by one or more orders, provide for all or any of the following matters, namely—

(a) the transfer in whole or in part of the assets, rights and liabilities of the existing Regional Council (including the rights and liabilities under any contract made by it) to the corresponding new District Council;

(b) the substitution of the corresponding new District Council or the existing Regional Council as a party to the legal proceedings to which the existing Regional Council is a party;

(c) the transfer or re-employment of any employees of the existing Regional Council to or by the corresponding new District Council the terms and conditions of service applicable to such employees after such transfer or re-employment;

(d) the continuance of any laws made by the existing Regional Council and in force immediately before the prescribed date, subject to such adaptations and modifications, whether by way of repeal or amendments, as the Administrator may make in this behalf until such laws are altered, repealed or amended by a competent Legislature or other competent authority.

(e) such incidental consequential and supplementary matters as the Administrator considers necessary.

20BB. Exercise of Discretionary Powers by the Governor in the Discharge of his Functions

The Governor, in the discharge of his functions under sub-paragraphs (2) and (3) of paragraph 1, sub-paragraphs (1) and (7) of paragraph 2, sub-paragraph (3) of paragraph 3, sub-paragraph (4) of paragraph 4, paragraph 5, sub-paragraph (1) of paragraph 6, sub-paragraph (2) of paragraph 7, sub-paragraph (3) of paragraph 9, sub-paragraph (1) of paragraph 14, sub-paragraph (1) of paragraph 15 and sub-paragraphs (1) and (2) of paragraph 16 of this Schedule, shall, after consulting the Council of Ministers, and if he thinks it necessary, the District Council or the Regional Council concerned, take such action as he considers necessary in his discretion.

20C. Interpretation

Subject to any provision made in this behalf, the provisions of this Schedule shall, in their application to the State of Mizoram, have effect—

(1) as if references to the Governor and Government of the State were references to the Administrator of the Union territory appointed under article 239, references to State (except in the expression "Government of the State") were references

to the Union territory of Mizoram and references to the State Legislature were references to the Legislative Assembly of the Union territory of Mizoram;

(2) as if—

(a) in sub-paragraph (5) of paragraph 4, the provision for consultation with the Government of the State concerned had been omitted;

(b) in sub-paragraph (2) of paragraph 6, for the words "to which the executive power of the State extends", the words "with respect to which the Legislative Assembly of the Union territory of Mizoram has power to make laws" had been substituted;

(c) in paragraph 13, the words and figures "under article 202" had been omitted.

21. Amendment of the Schedule

(1) Parliament may from time to time by law amend by way of addition, variation or repeal any of the provisions of this Schedule and, when the Schedule is so amended, any reference to this Schedule in this Constitution shall be construed as a reference to such Schedule as so amended.

(2) No such law as is mentioned in sub-paragraph (1) of this paragraph shall be deemed to be an amendment of this Constitution for the purposes of article 368.

4

Ninth Schedule to the Constitution

(Article 31B)

1. The Bihar Land Reforms Act, 1950 (Bihar Act XXX of 1950).
2. The Bombay Tenancy and Agricultural Lands Act, 1948 (Bombay Act LXVII of 1948).
3. The Bombay Maleki Tenure Abolition Act, 1949 (Bombay Act LXI of 1949).
4. The Bombay Taluqdari Tenure Abolition Act, 1949 (Bombay Act LXII of 1949).
5. The Panch Mahals Mehwassi Tenure Abolition Act, 1949 (Bombay Act LXIII of 1949).
6. The Bombay Khoti Abolition Act, 1950 (Bombay Act VI of 1950).
7. The Bombay Paragana and Kulkarni Watan Abolition Act, 1950 (Bombay Act LX of 1950).
8. The Madhya Pradesh Abolition of Proprietary Rights (Estates, Mahals, Alienated Lands) Act 1950 (Madhya Pradesh Act I of 1951).
9. The Madras Estates (Abolition and Conversion into Ryotwari) Amendment Act, 1948 (Madras Act I of 1948).
10. The Madras Estates (Abolition and Conversion into Ryotwari) Amendment Act, 1950 (Madras Act I of 1950).
11. The Uttar Pradesh Zamindari Abolition and Land Reforms Act, 1950 (Uttar Pradesh Act I of 1951).
12. The Hyderabad (Abolition of Jagirs) Regulation, 1358F. (No LXIX of 1358, Fasli)
13. The Hyderabad Jagirs (Communication) Regulation, 1359F. (No XXV of 1359, Fasli)

14. The Bihar Displaced Persons Rehabilitation (Acquisition of Land) Act, 1950 (Bihar Act XXXVIII of 1950).
15. The United Province Land Acquisition (Rehabilitation of Refugees) Act, 1948 (U.P. Act XXVI of 1948).
16. The Resettlement of Displaced Persons (Land Acquisition) Act, 1948 (Act LX of 1948).
17. Sections 52A to 52G of the Insurance Act, 1938 (Act IV of 1938) as inserted by section 42 of the Insurance (Amendment) Act, 1950 (Act XLVII of 1950).
18. The Railways Companies (Emergency Provisions) Act, 1951 (Act LI of 1951).
19. Chapter III-A of the Industries (Development and Regulation) Act, 1951 (Act LXV of 1951), as inserted by section 13, of the Industries (Development and Regulation) Amendment Act, 1953 (Act XXVI of 1953).
20. The West Bengal Land Development and Planning Act, 1948 (West Bengal Act XXI of 1948), as amended by West Bengal Act XXIX of 1951.
21. The Andhra Pradesh Ceiling on Agricultural Holding Act, 1961 (Andhra Pradesh X of 1961).
22. The Andhra Pradesh (Telangana Area) Tenancy and Agricultural Lands (Validation) Act, 1961 (Andhra Pradesh Act XXI of 1961).
23. The Andhra Pradesh (Telangana Area) Ijdra and Kowil Land Cancellation of Irregular Pattas and Abolition of Concessional Assessment Act, 1961 (Andhra Pradesh Act XXXVI of 1961).
24. The Assam State Acquisition of Lands Belonging to Religious or Charitable Institution of Public Nature Act, 1959 (Assam Act IX of 1961).
25. The Bihar Land Reforms (Amendment) Act, 1953 (Bihar Act XX of 1954).
26. The Bihar Land Reforms (Fixation of Ceiling Area and Acquisition of Surplus Land) Act, 1961 (Bihar Act XII of 1962). (except section 28 of this Act).

27. The Bombay Taluqdari Tenure Abolition (Amendment) Act,1954 (Bombay Act I of 1955).
28. The Bombay Taluqdari Tenure Abolition (Amendment) Act,1957 (Bombay Act XVIII of 1958).
29. The Bombay Imams (Kutch Area) Abolition Act,1958 (Bombay Act XCVIII of 1958).
30. The Bombay Tenancy and Agricultural Lands (Gujarat Amendment) Act,1960 (Gujarat Act XVI of 1960).
31. The Gujarat Agricultural Lands Ceiling Act, 1960 (Gujarat Act XXVIII of 1961).
32. The Sagbara and Mahwassi Estate (Proprietary Rights Abolition, etc.) Regulation, 1962 (Gujarat Regulation I of 1962).
33. The Gujarat Surviving Alienations Abolition Act, 1963 (Gujarat Act XXXIII of 1963). except insofar as this Act relates to an Alienation referred to in Sub-clause (d) of Clause (3) of Section 2 thereof.
34. The Maharashtra Agricultural Lands (Ceiling on Holdings) Act, 1961 (Maharashtra Act XXVII of 1961).
35. The Hyderabad Tenancy and Agricultural Lands (Re-enactment, Validation and Further Amendment) Act, 1961 (Maharashtra Act XLV of 1961).
36. The Hyderabad Tenancy and Agricultural Lands Act, 1950 (Hyderabad Act XXI of 1950).
37. The Jenmikaram Payment (Abolition) Act. 1960 (Kerala III of 1961)
38. The Kerala Land Tax Act, 1961 (Kerala Act XIII of 1961).
39. The Kerala Land Reforms Act, 1963 (Kerala Act I of 1964).
40. The Madhya Pradesh Land Revenue Code, 1959 (Madhya Pradesh Act XX of 1959).
41. The Madhya Pradesh Ceiling on Agricultural Holdings Act, 1960 (Madhya Pradesh Act XX of 1960).
42. The Madras Cultivating Tenants Protection Act, 1955 (Madras Act XXV of 1955).
43. The Madras Cultivating Tenants (Payment of Fair Rent) Act, 1956 (Madras Act XXIV of 1956).

44. The Madras Occupants of Kudiyiruppu (Protection from Eviction) Act, 1961 (Madras Act XXXVIII of 1961).
45. The Madras Public Trusts (Regulation of Administration of Agricultural Lands) Act, 1961 (Madras Act LVII of 1961).
46. The Madras Land Reforms (Fixation of Ceiling on Land) Act, 1961 (Madras Act LVII of 1961).
47. The Mysore Tenancy Act, 1952 (Mysore Act XII of 1952).
48. The Coorg Tenants Act, 1957 (Mysore Act XIV of 1957).
49. The Mysore Village Offices Abolition Act, 1961 (Mysore Act XIV of 1961)
50. The Hyderabad Tenancy and Agricultural Lands (Validation) Act, 1961 (Mysore Act XXXVI of 1961).
51. The Mysore Land Reforms Act, 1961 (Mysore Act X of 1962).
52. The Orissa Land Reforms Act, 1960 (Orissa Act XVI of 1960).
53. The Orissa Merged Territories (Village Office Abolition) Act, 1963 (Orissa Act X of 1963).
54. The Punjab Security of Land Tenures Act, 1953 (Punjab Act X of 1953).
55. The Rajasthan Tenancy Act, 1955 (Rajasthan Act III of 1955).
56. The Rajasthan Zamindari and Biswedari Abolition Act, 1959 (Rajasthan Act VIII of 1959).
57. The Kumaun and Uttarakhand Zamindari Abolition and Land Reforms Act, 1960 (Uttar Pradesh Act XVII of 1960).
58. The Uttar Pradesh Imposition of Ceiling on Land Holdings Act, 1960 (Uttar Pradesh Act I of 1961).
59. The West Bengal Estates Acquisition Act, 1953 (West Bengal Act I of 1954).
60. The West Bengal Land Reforms Act, 1955 (West Bengal Act X of 1956).
61. The Delhi Land Reforms Act, 1954 (Delhi Act VIII of 1954).
62. The Delhi Land Holdings (Ceiling) Act, 1960 (Central Act 24 of 1960).
63. The Manipur Land Revenue and Land Reforms Act, 1960 (Central Act 33 of 1960).

64. The Tripura Land Revenue and Land Reforms Act, 1960 (Central Act 33 of 1960).

Explanation: Any Acquisition made under the Rajasthan Tenancy Act, 1955 (Rajasthan Act III of 1955), in contravention of the second proviso to clause (1) of Article 31A shall, to the extent of contravention, be void.

65. The Kerala Land Reforms (Amendment) Act, 1969 (Kerala Act 35 of 1969).
66. The Kerala Land Reforms (Amendment) Act, 1971 (Kerala Act 25 of 1971).
67. The Andhra Pradesh Land Reforms (Ceilings on Agricultural Holdings) Act, 1973 (Andhra Pradesh Act I of 1973).
68. The Bihar Land Reforms (Fixation of Ceiling Areas and Acquisition of Surplus Land) (Amendment) Act, 1972 (Bihar Act IX of 1973).
69. The Bihar Land Reforms (Fixation of Ceiling Areas and Acquisition of Surplus Land) (Amendment) Act, 1973 (Bihar Act IX of 1973).
70. The Bihar Land Reforms (Amendment) Act, 1972 (Bihar Act V of 1972).
71. The Gujarat Agricultural Lands Ceiling (Amendment)Act, 1972 (Gujarat Act of 1974).
72. The Haryana Ceiling on Land Holdings Act, 1972 (Haryana Act 19 of 1972).
73. The Himachal Pradesh Ceiling on Land Holdings Act, 1972 (Himachal Pradesh Act 19 of 1973).
74. The Kerala Land Reforms (Amendment) Act, 1972 (Kerala Act 17 of 1972).
75. The Madhya Pradesh Ceiling on Agricultural Holdings, (Amendment) Act, 1972 (Madhya Pradesh Act 12 of 1974).
76. The Madhya Pradesh Ceiling on Agricultural Holdings, (Second Amendment) Act, 1972 (Madhya Pradesh Act 13 of 1974).

77. The Mysore Land Reforms (Amendment) Act, 1973 (Karnataka Act I of 1974).
78. The Punjab Land Reforms Act, 1972 (Punjab Act 10 of 1973).
79. The Rajasthan Imposition of Ceiling on Agricultural Holdings Act, 1973 (Rajasthan Act 11 of 1973).
80. The Gudalpur Janmam Estates (Abolition and Conversion into Ryotwari) Act, 1969 (Tamil Nadu Act 24 of 1969).
81. The West Bengal Land Reforms (Amendment) Act, 1972 (West Bengal Act XII of 1972).
82. The West Bengal Estates Acquisition (Amendment) Act, 1964 (West Bengal Act XXII of 1964).
83. The West Bengal Estates (Second Amendment) Act, 1973 (West Bengal Act XXXIII of 1973).
84. The Bombay Tenancy and Agricultural Lands (Gujarat Amendment) Act, 1972 (Gujarat Act 5 of 1973).
85. The Orissa Land Reforms (Amendment) Act, 1974 (Orissa Act 9 of 1974).
86. The Tripura Land Revenue and Land Reforms (Second Amendment) Act, 1974 (Tripura Act 7 of 1974).
87. Omitted by the 44th Amendment Act, 1976.
88. The Industries (Development and Regulation) Act, 1951 (Central Act 65 of 1951).
89. The Requisitioning and Acquisition of Immovable Property Act, 1952 (Central Act 30 of 1952).
90. The Mines and Minerals (Regulation and Development) Act, 1957 (Central Act 66 of 1957).
91. The Monopolies and Restrictive Trade Practices Act, 1969 (Central Act 54 of 1969).
92. Omitted by the Constitution (44th Amendment) Act, 1978.
93. The Coking Coal Mines (Emergency Provisions) Act, 1971 (Central Act 36 of 1971).
94. The Coking Coal Mines (Nationalisation) Act, 1972 (Central Act 36 of 1972).
95. The General Insurance Business (Nationalisation) Act, 1972 (Central Act 57 of 1972).

96. The Indian Copper Corporation (Acquisition of Undertaking) Act, 1972 (Central Act 58 of 1972).
97. The Sick Textile Undertakings (Taking Over of Management) Act, 1972 (Central Act 72 of 1972).
98. The Coal Mines (Taking Over of Management) Act, 1973 (Central Act 15 of 1973).
99. The Coal Mines (Nationalisation) Act, 1973 (Central Act 26 of 1973).
100. The Foreign Exchange Regulation Act, 1973 (Central Act 46 of 1973).
101. The Alcock Ashdown Company Limited (Aquisition of Undertaking) Act, 1973 (Central Act 56 of 1973).
102. The Coal Mines (Conservation and Development) Act, 1974 (Central Act 28 of 1974).
103. The Additional Emoluments (Compulsory Deposit) Act, 1974 (Central Act 37 of 1974).
104. The Conservation of Foreign Exchange and Prevention of Smuggling Activities Act, 1974 (Central Act 52 of 1974).
105. The Sick Textile Undertaking (Nationalisation) Act, 1974 (Central Act 57 of 1974).
106. The Maharashtra Agricultural Lands (Ceiling on Holdings) (Amendment) Act, 1965 (Maharashtra Act XVI of 1965).
107. The Maharashtra Agricultural Lands (Ceiling on Holdings) (Amendment) Act, 1965 (Maharashtra Act XXXVII of 1965).
108. The Maharashtra Agricultural Lands (Ceiling on Holdings) (Amendment) Act, 1968 (Maharashtra Act XVI of 1968).
109. The Maharashtra Agricultural Lands (Ceiling on Holdings) (Second Amendment) Act, 1968 (Maharashtra Act XXXIII of 1968).
110. The Maharashtra Agricultural Lands (Ceiling on Holdings) (Amendment) Act, 1969 (Maharashtra Act XXXVII of 1969).
111. The Maharashtra Agricultural Lands (Ceiling on Holdings) (Second Amendment) Act, 1969 (Maharashtra Act XXXVIII of 1969).

112. The Maharashtra Agricultural Lands (Ceiling on Holdings) (Amendment) Act, 1970 (Maharashtra Act XXVII of 1970)
113. The Maharashtra Agricultural Lands (Ceiling on Holdings) (Amendment) Act, 1970 (Maharashtra Act XIII of 1970).
114. The Maharashtra Agricultural Lands (Ceiling on Holdings) (Amendment) Act, 1973 (Maharashtra Act L of 1973).
115. The Orissa Land Reforms (Amendment) Act, 1965 (Orissa Act 13 of 1965).
116. The Orissa Land Reforms (Amendment) Act, 1966 (Orissa Act 8 of 1967).
117. The Orissa Land Reforms (Amendment) Act, 1967 (Orissa Act 13 of 1967).
118. The Orissa Land Reforms (Amendment) Act, 1969 (Orissa Act 13 of 1969).
119. The Orissa Land Reforms (Amendment) Act, 1970 (Orissa Act 18 of 1970).
120. The Uttar Pradesh Imposition of Ceiling on Land Holdings (Amendment) Act, 1972 (Uttar Pradesh Act 18 of 1973).
121. The Uttar Pradesh Imposition of Ceiling on Land Holdings (Amendment) Act, 1974 (Uttar Pradesh Act 2 of 1975).
122. The Tripura Land Revenue and Land Reforms (Third Amendment) Act, 1975 (Tripura Act 3 of 1975).
123. The Dadra and Nagar Haveli Land Reforms Regulation, 1971, (3 of 1971).
124. The Dadra and Nagar Haveli Land Reforms (Amendment) Regulation, 1973, (5 of 1973).
125. Section 66A and Chapter IV-A of the Motor Vehicles Act, 1939 (Central Act 4 of 1973).
126. The Essential Commodities Act, 1955 (Central Act 10 of 1955).
127. The Smugglers and Foreign Exchange Manipulators (Forfeiture of Property) Act, 1976 (Central Act 13 of 1976).
128. The Bonded Labour System (Abolition) Act, 1976 (Central Act of 19 of 1976).
129. The Conservation of Foreign Exchange and Prevention of

Smuggling Activities (Amendment) Act, 1976 (Central Act 20 of 1976).

130. Omitted by the 44th Amendment Act, 1976.

131. The Levy Sugar Price Equalisation Fund Act, 1976 (Central Act 31 of 1976).

132. The Urban Land (Ceiling and Regulation) Act, 1976 (Central Act 33 of 1976).

133. The Departmentalization of Union Accounts (Transfer of Personnel) Act, 1976 (Central Act 59 of 1976).

134. The Assam Fixation of Ceiling on Land Holdings Act, 1956 (Assam Act 1 of 1957).

135. The Bombay Tenancy and Agricultural Lands (Vidarbha Region) Act, 1958 (Bombay Act XCIX of 1958).

136. The Gujarat Private Forests (Acquisition) Act, 1972 (Gujarat Act 14 of 1973).

137. The Haryana Ceiling on Land Holdings (Amendment) Act, 1976 (Haryana Act 17 of 1976).

138. The Himachal Pradesh Tenancy and Land Reforms Act, 1972 (Himachal Pradesh Act 8 of 1974).

139. The Himachal Pradesh Village Common Lands Vesting and Utilization Act, 1974 (Himachal Pradesh Act 18 of 1974).

140. The Karnataka Land Reforms (Second Amendment and Miscellaneous Provisions) Act, 1974 (Karnataka Act 31 of 1974).

141. The Karnataka Land Reforms (Second Amendment Provisions) Act, 1976 (Karnataka Act 27 of 1976).

142. The Kerala Prevention of Eviction Act, 1966 (Kerala Act 12 of 1966).

143. The Thiruppuvaram Payment (Abolition) Act, 1969 (Kerala Act 19 of 1969).

144. The Sreepadam Lands Enfranchisement Act, 1969 (Kerala Act 20 of 1969).

145. The Sree Pandaravaka Lands (Vesting and Enfranchisement) Act, 1971 (Kerala Act 20 of 1971).

146. The Kerala Private Forests (Vesting and Assignment) Act, 1971 (Kerala Act 26 of 1971).

147. The Kerala Agricultural Workers Act, 1974 (Kerala Act 18 of 1974).
148. The Kerala Cashew Factories (Acquisition) Act, 1974 (Kerala Act 29 of 1974).
149. The Kerala Chitties Act, 1975 (Kerala Act 23 of 1975).
150. The Kerala Scheduled Tribes (Restriction on Transfer of Lands and Restoration of Alienated Lands) Act, 1975 (Kerala Act 31 of 1975).
151. The Kerala Land Reforms (Amendment) Act, 1976 (Kerala Act 15 of 1976).
152. The Kanam Tenancy Act, 1976 (Kerala Act 16 of 1976).
153. The Madhya Pradesh Ceiling on Agricultural Holdings (Amendment) Act, 1974 (Madhya Pradesh Act 20 of 1974).
154. The Madhya Pradesh Ceiling on Agricultural Holdings (Amendment) Act, 1975 (Madhya Pradesh Act 2 of 1975).
155. The West Khandesh Mehwassi Estates (Proprietary Rights Abolition, etc.) Regulation, 1961 (Maharashtra Regulation I of 1962).
156. The Maharashtra Restoration of Lands to Scheduled Tribes Act, 1974 (Maharashtra Act XIV of 1975).
157. The Maharashtra Agricultural Lands (Lowering of Ceiling on Holdings) and (Amendment) Act, 1972 (Maharashtra Act XXI of 1975)
158. The Maharashtra Private Forests (Acquisition) Act, 1975 (Maharashtra Act XXXIX of 1975).
159. The Maharashtra Agricultural Lands (Lowering of Ceiling on Holdings) and (Amendment) Act, 1975 (Maharashtra Act XLVII of 1975).
160. The Maharashtra Agricultural Lands (Ceiling on Holdings) and (Amendment) Act, 1975 (Maharashtra Act II of 1976).
161. The Orissa Estates Abolition Act, 1951 (Orissa Act I of 1952)
162. The Rajasthan Colonization Act, 1954 (Rajasthan Act XXVII of 1954).
163. The Rajasthan Land Reforms and Acquisition of Land-owners' Estates Act, 1963 (Rajasthan Act II of 1964).

164. The Rajasthan Imposition of Ceiling on Agricultural Holdings (Amendment) Act, 1976 (Rajasthan Act 8 of 1976).
165. The Rajasthan Tenancy Act (Amendment) Act, 1976.
166. The Tamil Nadu Land Reforms (Reduction of Ceiling on Land) Amendment Act, 1970 (Tamil Nadu Act 17 of 1970).
167. The Tamil Nadu Land Reforms (Fixation of Ceiling on Land) Amendment Act, 1971 (Tamil Nadu Act 41 of 1971).
168. The Tamil Nadu Land Reforms (Fixation of Ceiling on Land) Amendment Act, 1972 (Tamil Nadu Act 10 of 1972).
169. The Tamil Nadu Land Reforms (Fixation of Ceiling on Land) Amendment Act, 1972 (Tamil Nadu Act 20 of 1972).
170. The Tamil Nadu Land Reforms (Fixation of Ceiling on Land) Third Amendment Act, 1972 (Tamil Nadu Act 37 of 1972).
171. The Tamil Nadu Land Reforms (Fixation of Ceiling on Land) Fourth Amendment Act, 1972 (Tamil Nadu Act 39 of 1972).
172. The Tamil Nadu Land Reforms (Fixation of Ceiling on Land) Sixth Amendment Act, 1972 (Tamil Nadu Act 7 of 1972).
173. The Tamil Nadu Land Reforms (Fixation of Ceiling on Land) Fifth Amendment Act, 1972 (Tamil Nadu Act 10 of 1972).
174. The Tamil Nadu Land Reforms (Fixation of Ceiling on Land) Amendment Act, 1974 (Tamil Nadu Act 15 of 1974).
175. The Tamil Nadu Land Reforms (Fixation of Ceiling on Land) Third Amendment Act, 1974 (Tamil Nadu Act 30 of 1974).
176. The Tamil Nadu Land Reforms (Fixation of Ceiling on Land) Second Amendment Act, 1974 (Tamil Nadu Act 32 of 1974).
177. The Tamil Nadu Land Reforms (Fixation of Ceiling on Land) Amendment Act, 1975 (Tamil Nadu Act 11 of 1975).
178. The Tamil Nadu Land Reforms (Fixation of Ceiling on Land) Second Amendment Act, 1975 (Tamil Nadu Act 21 of 1975).
179. Amendments made to the Uttar Pradesh Zamindari Abolition and Land Reform Act, 1950 (Uttar Pradesh Act 1 of 1951) by the Uttar Pradesh Land Laws (Amendment) Act, 1971 (Uttar Pradesh Act 21 of 1971) and the Uttar Pradesh Land Laws (Amendment) Act, 1974 (Uttar Pradesh Act 34 of 1974).

180. The Uttar Pradesh Imposition of Ceiling on Land Holdings (Amendment) Act, 1976 (Uttar Pradesh Act 20 of 1976).
181. The West Bengal Land Reforms (Second Amendment) Act, 1972 (West Bengal Act XXVIII of 1972).
182. The West Bengal Restoration of Alienated Land Act, 1973 (West Bengal Act XXIII of 1973).
183. The West Bengal Land Reforms (Amendment) Act, 1974 (West Bengal Act XXXIII of 1974).
184. The West Bengal Land Reforms (Amendment) Act, 1975 (West Bengal Act XXIII of 1975).
185. The West Bengal Land Reforms (Amendment) Act, 1976 (West Bengal Act XII of 1976).
186. The Delhi Land Holdings (Ceiling) Amendment Act, 1976 (Central Act 15 of 1976).
187. The Goa, Daman and Diu Mandkars (Protection from Eviction) Act, 1975 (Goa, Daman and Diu Act 1 of 1976).
188. The Pondicherry Land Reforms (Fixation of Ceiling on Land) Act, 1973 (Pondicherry Act 9 of 1974).
189. The Assam (Temporarily Settled Areas) Tenancy Act, 1971 (Assam Act XXIII of 1971).
190. The Assam (Temporarily Settled Areas) Tenancy (Amendment) Act, 1974 (Assam Act XVIII of 1974).
191. The Bihar Land Reforms (Fixation of Ceiling Area and Acquisition of Surplus Land) (Amendment) Act, 1974 (Bihar Act 13 of 1975).
192. The Bihar Land Reforms (Fixation of Ceiling Area and Acquisition of Surplus Land) (Amendment Amending) Act, 1976 (Bihar Act 22 of 1976).
193. The Bihar Land Reforms (Fixation of Ceiling Area and Acquisition of Surplus Land) (Amendment Amending) Act, 1978 (Bihar Act VII of 1978).
194. The Land Acquisition (Bihar Amendment) Act, 1979 (Bihar Act 2 of 1980).
195. The Haryana Ceiling on Land Holdings (Amendment) Act, 1977 (Haryana Act 14 of 1977).

196. The Tamil Nadu Land Reforms (Fixation of Ceiling on Land) Amendment Act, 1978 (Tamil Nadu Act 25 of 1978).
197. The Tamil Nadu Land Reforms (Fixation of Ceiling on Land) Amendment Act, 1979 (Tamil Nadu Act 11 of 1979).
198. The Uttar Pradesh Zamindari Abolition Laws (Amendment) Act, 1978 (Uttar Pradesh Act 15 of 1978).
199. The West Bengal Restoration of Alienated Land (Amendment) Act, 1978 (West Bengal Act XXIV of 1978).
200. The West Bengal Restoration of Alienated Land (Amendment) Act, 1980 (West Bengal Act LVI of 1980).
201. The Goa, Daman and Diu Agricultural Tenancy Act, 1964 (Goa, Daman and Diu Act 7 of 1964).
202. The Goa, Daman and Diu Agricultural Tenancy (Fifth Amendment) Act, 1976 (Goa, Daman and Diu Act 17 of 1976).
203. The Andhra Pradesh Scheduled Areas Land Transfer Regulation, 1959, (Andhra Pradesh Regulation 1 of 1959).
204. The Andhra Pradesh Scheduled Areas Laws (Extension and Amendment) Regulation, 1963 (Andhra Pradesh Regulation 2 of 1963).
205. The Andhra Pradesh Scheduled Areas Land Transfer (Amendment) Regulation, 1970, (Andhra Pradesh Regulation 1 of 1970).
206. The Andhra Pradesh Scheduled Areas Land Transfer (Amendment) Regulation, 1971 (Andhra Pradesh Regulation 1 of 1971).
207. The Andhra Pradesh Scheduled Areas Land Transfer (Amendment) Regulation, 1978, (Andhra Pradesh Regulation 1 of 1978).
208. The Bihar Tenancy Act, 1885 (Bihar Act 8 of 1885).
209. The Chota Nagpur Tenancy Act, 1908 (Bengal Act 6 of 1908) (Chapter VIII Sections 46, 47, 48, 48-A and 49; Chapter X, Sections 71, 71-A and 71-B; Chapter XVIII, Sections 240, 241 and 242).
210. The Santhal Parganas Tenancy (Supplementary Provisions) Act, 1949 (Bihar Act 14 of 1949) Except Sections 53.

211. The Bihar Scheduled Areas Regulation, 1969 (Bihar Regulation 1 of 1969).
212. The Bihar Land Reforms (Fixation of Ceiling Area and Acquisition of Surplus Land) (Amendment) Act, 1982 (Bihar Act 55 of 1982).
213. The Gujarat Devasthan Inams Abolition Act, 1969, (Gujarat Act 16 of 1969).
214. The Gujarat Tenancy Laws (Amendment) Act, 1976, (Gujarat Act 37 of 1976).
215. The Gujarat Agricultural Lands Ceiling (Amendment) Act, 1976 (President's Act 43 of 1976).
216. The Gujarat Devasthan Inams Abolition (Amendment) Act, 1977, (Gujarat Act 27 of 1977).
217. The Gujarat Tenancy Laws (Amendment) Act, 1977, (Gujarat Act 30 of 1977).
218. The Bombay Land Revenue (Gujarat Second Amendment) Act, 1980 (Gujarat Act 37 of 1980).
219. The Bombay Land Revenue Code and Land Tenure Abolition Laws (Gujarat Amendment) Act, 1982 (Gujarat Act 8 of 1982).
220. The Himachal Pradesh Transfer of Land (Regulation) Act, 1968 (Himachal Pradesh Act 15 of 1969).
221. The Himachal Pradesh Transfer of Land (Regulation) (Amendment) Act, 1986 (Himachal Pradesh Act 16 of 1986).
222. The Karnataka Scheduled Castes and Scheduled Tribes (Prohibition of Transfer of Certain Lands) Act, 1978 (Karnataka Act 1 of 1979).
223. The Kerala Land Reforms (Amendment) Act, 1978 (Kerala Act 13 of 1978).
224. The Kerala Land Reforms (Amendment) Act, 1981 (Kerala Act 19 of 1981).
225. The Madhya Pradesh Land Revenue Code (Third Amendment) Act, 1976 (Madhya Pradesh Act 61 of 1976).
226. The Madhya Pradesh Land Revenue Code (Amendment) Act, 1980 (Madhya Pradesh Act 15 of 1980).

227. The Madhya Pradesh Akrishik Jot Uchchatam Seema Adhiniyam, 1981 (Madhya Pradesh Act 11 of 1981).
228. The Madhya Pradesh Ceiling on Agricultural Holdings (Second Amendment) Act, 1976 (Madhya Pradesh Act 1 of 1984).
229. The Madhya Pradesh Ceiling on Agricultural Holdings (Amendment) Act, 1984 (Madhya Pradesh Act 14 of 1984).
230. The Madhya Pradesh Ceiling on Agricultural Holdings (Amendment) Act, 1989 (Madhya Pradesh Act 8 of 1989).
231. The Maharashtra Land Revenue Code, 1966 (Maharashtra Act 41 of 1966), Sections 36, 36-A and 36-B.
232. The Maharashtra Land Revenue Code and the Maharashtra Restoration of Lands to Scheduled Tribes (Second Amendment) Act, 1976 (Maharashtra Act 30 of 1977).
233. The Maharashtra Abolition of Subsisting Proprietary Rights to Mines and Minerals in Certain Lands Act, 1985 (Maharashtra Act 16 of 1985).
234. The Orissa Schedule Areas Transfer of Immovable Property (By Scheduled Tribes) Regulation, 1956 (Orissa Regulation 2 of 1956).
235. The Orissa Land Reforms (Second Amendment) Act, 1975 (Orissa Act 29 of 1976).
236. The Orissa Land Reforms (Amendment) Act, 1976 (Orissa Act 30 of 1976).
237. The Orissa Land Reforms (Second Amendment) Act, 1976 (Orissa Act 44 of 1976).
238. The Rajasthan Colonisation (Amendment) Act, 1984 (Rajasthan Act 12 of 1984).
239. The Rajasthan Tenancy (Amendment) Act, 1984 (Rajasthan Act 13 of 1984).
240. The Rajasthan Tenancy (Amendment) Act, 1987 (Rajasthan Act 21 of 1987).
241. The Tamil Nadu Land Reforms (Fixation of Ceiling on Land) Second Amendment Act, 1979 (Tamil Nadu Act 8 of 1980).
242. The Tamil Nadu Land Reforms (Fixation of Ceiling on Land) Amendment Act, 1980 (Tamil Nadu Act 21 of 1980).

243. The Tamil Nadu Land Reforms (Fixation of Ceiling on Land) Second Amendment Act, 1981 (Tamil Nadu Act 59 of 1981).
244. The Tamil Nadu Land Reforms (Fixation of Ceiling on Land) Second Amendment Act, 1983 (Tamil Nadu Act 2 of 1984).
245. The Uttar Pradesh Land Laws (Amendment) Act, 1982 (Uttar Pradesh Act 20 of 1982).
246. The West Bengal Land Reforms (Amendment) Act, 1965 (West Bengal Act 18 of 1965).
247. The West Bengal Land Reforms (Amendment) Act, 1966 (West Bengal Act 11 of 1966).
248. The West Bengal Land Reforms (Second Amendment) Act, 1969 (West Bengal Act 23 of 1969).
249. The West Bengal Estate Acquisition (Amendment) Act, 1977 (West Bengal Act 36 of 1977).
250. The West Bengal Land Holding Revenue Act, 1979 (West Bengal Act 44 of 1979).
251. The West Bengal Land Reforms (Amendment) Act, 1980 (West Bengal Act 41 of 1980).
252. The West Bengal Land Holding Revenue (Amendment) Act, 1981 (West Bengal Act 33 of 1981).
253. The Calcutta Thikka Tenancy (Acquisition and Regulation) Act, 1981 (West Bengal Act 37 of 1981).
254. The West Bengal Land Holding Revenue (Amendment) 1982 (West Bengal Act 23 of 1982).
255. The Calcutta Thikka Tenancy (Acquisition and Regulation) (Amendment) Act, 1984 (West Bengal Act 41 of 1984)
256. The Mahe Land Reforms Act, 1968 (Pondicherry Act 1 of 1968).
257. The Mahe Land Reforms (Amendment) Act, 1980 (Pondicherry Act 1 of 1981).

257A. The Tamil Nadu Backward Classes, Scheduled Castes and Scheduled Tribes (Reservation of Seats in Educational Institutions and of appointments or posts in the Services under the State) Act, 1993 (Tamil Nadu Act 45 of 1994).

258. The Bihar Privileged Persons Homestead Tenancy Act, 1947 (Bihar Act 4 of 1948).

259. The Bihar Consolidation of Holdings and Prevention of Fragmentation Act, 1956 (Bihar Act 22 of 1956).
260. The Bihar Consolidation of Holdings and Prevention of Fragmentation (Amendment) Act, 1970 (Bihar Act 7 of 1970).
261. The Bihar Privileged Persons Homestead Tenancy (Amendment) Act, 1970 (Bihar Act 9 of 1970).
262. The Bihar Consolidation of Holdings and Prevention of Fragmentation (Amendment) Act, 1973 (Bihar Act 35 of 1982).
263. The Bihar Consolidation of Holdings and Prevention of Fragmentation (Amendment) Act, 1981 (Bihar Act 35 of 1982).
264. The Bihar Land Reforms (Fixation of Ceiling Area and Acquisition of Surplus Land) (Amendment) Act, 1987 (Bihar Act 21 of 1987).
265. The Bihar Privileged Persons Homestead Tenancy (Amendment) Act, 1989 (Bihar Act 11 of 1989).
266. The Bihar Land Reforms (Amendment) Act, 1989 (Bihar Act 11 of 1990).
267. The Karnataka Scheduled Castes and Scheduled Tribes (Prohibition of Transfer of Certain Lands) (Amendment) Act, 1984 (Karnataka Act 3 of 1984).
268. The Kerala Land Reforms (Amendment) Act, 1989 (Kerala Act 16 of 1989).
269. The Kerala Land Reforms (Second Amendment) Act, 1989 (Kerala Act 2 of 1990).
270. The Orissa Land Reforms (Amendment) Act, 1989 (Orissa Act 9 of 1990).
271. The Rajasthan Tenancy (Amendment) Act, 1979 (Rajasthan Act 16 of 1979).
272. The Rajasthan Colonisation (Amendment) Act, 1987 (Rajasthan Act 2 of 1987).
273. The Rajasthan Colonisation (Amendment) Act, 1989 (Rajasthan Act 12 of 1989).

274. The Tamil Nadu Land Reforms (Fixation of Ceiling on Land) Amendment Act, 1983 (Tamil Nadu Act 3 of 1984).
275. The Tamil Nadu Land Reforms (Fixation of Ceiling on Land) Amendment Act, 1983 (Tamil Nadu Act 57 of 1986).
276. The Tamil Nadu Land Reforms (Fixation of Ceiling on Land) Second Amendment Act, 1987 (Tamil Nadu Act 4 of 1988).
277. The Tamil Nadu Land Reforms (Fixation of Ceiling on Land) Amendment Act, 1989 (Tamil Nadu Act 30 of 1989).
278. The West Bengal Land Reforms (Amendment) Act, 1981 (West Bengal Act 50 of 1981).
279. The West Bengal Land Reforms (Amendment) Act, 1986 (West Bengal Act 5 of 1986).
280. The West Bengal Land Reforms (Second Amendment) Act, 1986 (West Bengal Act 19 of 1986).
281. The West Bengal Land Reforms (Third Amendment) Act, 1986 (West Bengal Act 19 of 1986).
282. The West Bengal Land Reforms (Amendment) Act, 1989 (West Bengal Act 23 of 1989).
283. The West Bengal Land Reforms (Amendment) Act, 1990 (West Bengal Act 24 of 1990).
284. The West Bengal Land Reforms Tribunal Act, 1991 (West Bengal Act 12 of 1991).

Explanation: Any Acquisition made under the Rajasthan Tenancy Act, 1955 (Rajasthan Act of 1955), in contravention of the second proviso to clause (1) of article 31A, shall, to the extent of the contravention, be void.

APPENDICES

APPENDIX – I

The Protection of Civil Rights Act, 1955

(Act No. 22 of 1955)

[8th May, 1955]

An Act to prescribe punishment for the [1][preaching and practice of "Untouchability"] for the enforcement of any disability arising therefrom and for matters connected therewith.

BE it enacted by Parliament in the Sixth Year of the Republic of India as follows:-

1. Short Title, Extent and Commencement

(1) This Act may be called [2][the Protection of Civil Rights Act], 1955.

(2) It extends[3] to the whole of India.

(3) It shall come into force on such date[4] as the Central Government may, by notification in the Official Gazette, appoint.

2. Definitions

In this Act, unless the context otherwise requires,–

---

1. Subs. by Act 106 of 1976, s. 2, for "practice of Untouchability" (w.e.f. 19-11-1976).
2. Subs. by s. 3, *ibid.*, for "the Untouchability (Offences) Act" (w.e.f. 19.11.1976).
3. Extended to Goa, Daman and Diu with modification by Regulation 12 of 1962, section 3 and Schedule to Dadra and Nagar Haveli by Regulation 6 of 1963, section 2 and Schedule I (w.e.f. 1st July, 1965) and to Pondicherry by Regulation 7 of 1963, section 3 and Schedule I (w.e.f. 1st October, 1963).
4. 1st June, 1955 vide notification No. S.R.O. 1109, dated 23rd May, 1955. *Gazette of India, 1955, Extraordinary, Part II, Section 3*, Page 1971.

[5][(a) "civil rights" means any right accruing to a person by reason of the abolition of "untouchability" by article 17 of the Constitution;]

[6][(aa) "hotel" includes a refreshment room, a boarding house, a lodging house, a coffee house and cafe;

[7][(b) "place" includes a house, building and other structure and premises; and also includes a tent, vehicle and vesssel;]

(c) "place of public entertainment" includes any place to which the public are admitted and in which an entertainment is provided or held.

Explanation – "Entertainment" includes any exhibition, performance, game sport and any other form of amusement;

(d) "place of public worship" means a place, by whatever name known, which is used as a place of public religious worship or which is dedicated generally to, or is used generally by, persons professing any religion or belonging to any religious denomination or any section thereof, for the performance of any religious service, or for offering prayers therein; [8][and includes–

(i) all lands subsidiary shrines appurtenant or attached to any such place,

(ii) a privately owned place of worship which is in fact, allowed by the owner thereof to be used as a place of public worship, and

(iii) such land or subsidiary shrine appurtenant to such privately owned place of worship as is allowed by the owner thereof to be used as a place of public religious worship;]

---

5. Ins. by Act 106 of 1976, s. 4 (w.e.f. 19-11-1976).
6. Clause (a) was relettered as clause (aa) by s. 4, *ibid.*, (w.e.f. 19-11-1976).
7. Subs. by s. 4 *ibid.*, for cl. (b) (w.e.f. 19-11-1976).
8. Subs. by Act 106 of 1976, s.4 for certain words (w.e.f 19.11.1976).

[9][(da) "prescribed" means prescribed by rules made under this Act;

(db) "Scheduled Castes" has the meaning assigned to it in clause (24) of article 366 of the Constitution;]

(e) "shop" means any premises where goods are sold either wholesale or by retail or both wholesale and by retail [8][and includes-

(i) any place from where goods are sold by a hawker or vendor or from a mobile van or cart;

(ii) a laundry and a hair cutting saloon;

(iii) any other place where services are rendered to customers.]

3. Punishment for Enforcing Religious Disabilities

Whoever on the ground of "untouchability" prevents any person–

(a) from entering any place of public worship which is open to other persons professing the same religion [10]*** of any section thereof, as such person; or

(b) from worshipping or offering prayers or performing any religious service in any place of public worship, or bathing in, or using the waters of, any sacred tank, well, spring or water-course [11][river or lake or bathing at any ghat of such tank, water-course, river or lake] in the same manner and to the same extent as is permissible to the other persons professing the same religion[10]*** or any section thereof, as such person;

[12][shall be punishable with imprisonment for a term of not less than one month and not more than six months and also with fine which shall be not less than one hundred rupees and not more than five hundred rupees].

---

9. Ins. by Act 106 of 1976; s. 4 (w.e.f. 19-11-1976).

10. The words "or belonging to the same religious denomination" omitted by s. 5, *ibid.*, w.e.f. 19-11-1976).

11. Ins. by s. 5, *ibid.*, (w.e.f. 19.11.1976).

12. Subs. by s. 5, *ibid.*, for certain words (w.e.f. 19.11.1976).

Explanation – For the purposes of this section and section 4 persons professing the Buddhist, Sikh or Jaina religion or persons professing the Hindu religion in any of its forms or developments including Virashaivas, Lingayats, Adivasis, followers of Brahmo, Prarthana, Arya Samaj and the Swaminarayan Sampraday shall be deemed to be Hindus.

4. Punishment for Enforcing Social Disabilities

Whoever on the ground of "untouchability" enforces against any person any disability with regard to–

(i) access to any shop, public restaurant, hotel or place of public entertainment; or

(ii) the use of any utensils, and other articles kept in any public restaurant, hotel, *dharamshala, sarai* or *musafirkhana* for the use of the general public or of [13][any section thereof]; or

(iii) the practice of any profession or the carrying on of any occupation, trade or business [14][or employment in any job]; or

(iv) the use of, or access to, any river, stream, spring, well, tank, cistern water-tap or other watering place, or any bathing ghat, burial or cremation ground, any sanitary convenience, any road, or passage, or any other place of public resort which other members of the public, or [13][any section thereof], have a right to use or have access to; or

(v) the use of, or access to , any place used for a charitable or a public purpose maintained wholly or partly out of State funds or dedicated to the use of the general public or [13][any section thereof]; or

(vi) the enjoyment of any benefit under a charitable trust created for the benefit of the general public or of [13][any section thereof]; or

(vii) the use of, or access to, any public conveyance; or

(viii) the construction, acquisition, or occupation of any residential premises in any locality, whatsoever; or

---

13. Subs. of Act 106 of 1976, s. 6 for certain words (w.e.f. 19-11-1976).
14. Ins. by s. 6 *ibid.*, (w.e.f. 19-11-1976).

(ix) the use of any *dharamshala, sarai* or *musafirkhana* which is open to the general public, or to [15][any section thereof]; or

(x) the observance of any social or religious custom, usage or ceremony or [16][taking part in, or taking out, any religious, social or cultural procession]; or

(xi) the use of jewellery and finery;

[17][shall be punishable with imprisonment for a term not less than one month and not more than six months and also with fine which shall be not less than one hundred rupees and not more than five hundred rupees].

[18][*Explanation*–For the purposes of this section, "enforcement of any disability" includes any discrimination on the ground of "untouchability".]

5. Punishment for Refusing to Admit Persons to Hospitals, etc. Whoever on the ground of "untouchability"–

(a) refuses admission to any person to any hospital, dispensary, educational institution or any hostel [19]* * * if such hospital, dispensary, educational institution or hostel is established or maintained for the benefit of the general public or any section thereof; or

(b) does any act which discriminates against any such person after admission to any of the aforesaid institutions;

[20][shall be punishable with imprisonment for a term of not less than one month and not more than six months and also with fine which shall be not less than one hundred rupees and not more than five hundred rupccs].

---

15. Subs. by Act of 106 of 1976, s. 6 for certain words (w.e.f. 19-11-1976)
16. Subs. by s. 6 *ibid.*, for "taking part in any religious procession" (w.e.f.19-11-1976).
17. Subs. by s. 7, *ibid.*, for certain words (w.e.f.19-11-1976).
18. Ins. by s. 6 *ibid.*, (w.e.f. 19-11-1976).
19. The words "attached thereto" omitted by s. 7, *ibid.*, (w.e.f. 19-11-1976).
20. Subs. by Act 106 of 1976, s. 7, for certain words (w.e.f. 19-11-1976).

6. Punishment for Refusing to Sell Goods or Render Services

Whosoever on the ground of "untouchability" refuses to sell any goods or refuses to render any service to any person at the same time and place and on the same terms and conditions at or which such goods are sold or services are rendered to other persons in the ordinary course of business [21][shall be punishable with imprisonment for a term of not less than one month and not more than six months and also with fine which shall be not less than one hundred rupees and not more than five hundred rupees].

7. Punishment for Other Offences arising out of "Untouchability"

(1) Whoever–

(a) prevents any person from exercising any right accruing to him by reason of the abolition of "untouchability" under article 17 of the Constitution; or

(b) molests, injures, annoys, obstructs or causes or attempts to cause obstruction to any person in the exercise of any such right or molests, injures, annoys or boycotts any person by reason of his having exercised any such right; or

(c) by words, either spoken or written, or by signs or by visible representations or otherwise, incites or encourages any person or class of persons or the public generally to practise "untouchability" in any form whatsoever;[22][or]

[22][(d) insults or attempts to insult, on the ground of "untouchability"a member of a Scheduled Caste],

[23][shall be punishable with imprisonment for a term of not less than one month and not more than six months, and also with fine which shall be not less than one hundred rupees and not more than five hundred rupees].

---

21. Subs. by s. 8, *ibid.*, for certain words (w.e.f. 19-11-1976).
22. Ins. by s. 9, *ibid.*, (w.e.f. 19-11-1976).
23. Subs. by *ibid.*, s. 9 for certain words (w.e.f. 19-11-1976).

[24][*Explanation* 1]- A person shall be deemed to boycott another person who-

(a) refuses to let to such other person or refuses to permit such other person, to use or occupy any house or land or refuses to deal with, work for hire for, or do business with, such other person or to render to him or receive from him any customary service, or refuses to do any of the said things on the terms on which such things would be commonly done in the ordinary course of business; or

(b) abstains from such social, professional or business relations as he would ordinarily maintain with such other person.

[25][*Explanation II*– For the purpose of clause (c) a person shall be deemed to incite or encourage the practice of "untouchability"—

(i) if he, directly or indirectly, preaches "untouchability" or its practice in any form; or

(ii) if he justifies, whether on historical, philosophical or religious grounds or on the grounds of any tradition of the caste system or on any other ground, the practice of "untouchability" in any form.]

[25][1A– Whoever commits any offences against the person or property of any individual as a reprisal or revenge for his having exercised any right accruing to him by reason of the abolition of "untouchability" under Article 17 of the Constitution, shall, where the offence is punishable with imprisonment for a term exceeding two years, be punishable with imprisonment for a term which shall not be less than two years and also with fine.]

---

24. Renumbered by s. 9, *ibid.*, (w.e.f. 19-11-1976).
25. Ins. by Act, 106 of 1976, s. 9 (w.e.f. 19-11-1976).

(2) Whoever–

(i) denies to any person belonging to his community or any section thereof any right or privilege to which such person would be entitled as a member of such community or section, or

(ii) takes any part in the ex-communication of such person, on the ground that such person has refused to practise "untouchability" or that such person has done any act in furtherance of the objects of this Act,

[26][shall be punishable with imprisonment for a term of not less than one month and not more than six months, and also with fine which shall not be less than one hundred rupees and not more than five hundred rupees],

[27][**7A. Unlawful Compulsory Labour when to be deemed to be a Practice of "Untouchability"**

(1) Whoever compels any person, on the ground of "untouchability" to do any scavenging or sweeping or to remove any carcass or to flay any animal or to remove the umbilical cord or to do any other job of a similar nature, shall be deemed to have enforced a disability arising out of "untouchability".

(2) Whoever is deemed under sub-section *(1)* to have enforced a disability arising out of "untouchability" shall be punishable with imprisonment for a term which shall not be less than three months and not more than six months and also with fine which shall not be less than one hundred rupees and not more than five hundred rupees.

Explanation – For the purposes of this section, "compulsion" includes a threat of social or economic boycott.]

---

26. Subs. by s. 9, *ibid.*, for certain words (w.e.f. 19-11-1976).
27. Ins. by s. 10, *ibid.*, (w.e.f. 19-11-1976).

8. Cancellation or Suspension of Licences in Certain Cases

When a person who is convicted of an offence under Section 6 holds any licence under any law for the time being in force in respect of any profession, trade, calling or employment in relation to which the offence is committed, the court trying the offence may, without prejudice to any other penalty to which such person may be liable under that section, direct that the licence shall stand cancelled or be suspended for such period as the court may deem fit, and every order of the court so cancelling or suspending a licence shall have effect as if it had been passed by the authority competent to cancel or suspend the licence under any such law.

Explanation– In this section, "licence" includes a permit or a permission.

9. Resumption or Suspension of Grants made by Government

Where the manager or trustee of a place of public worship [28][or any educational institution or hostel] which is in receipt of a grant of land or money from the Government is convicted of an offence under this Act and such conviction is not reversed or quashed in any appeal or revision, the Government may, if in its opinion the circumstances of the case warrant such a course, direct the suspension or resumption of the whole or any part of such grant.

10. Abetment of Offence

Whoever abets any offence under this Act shall be punishable with the punishment provided for the offence.

[29][*Explanation* – A public servant who wilfully neglects the investigation of any offence punishable under this Act shall be deemed to have abetted an offence punishable under this Act.]

---

28. Ins. by Act 106 of 1976, s. 11 (w.e.f. 19-11-1976).
29. Ins. by s. 12, *ibid.*, (w.e.f. 19-11-1976).

[30][**10A. Power of State Government to Impose Collective Fine**

(1) If, after an inquiry in the prescribed manner, the State Government is satisfied that the inhabitants of an area are concerned in, or abetting the commission of, any offence punishable under this Act, or harbouring persons concerned in the commission of such offence or failing to render all the assistance in their power to discover or apprehend the offender or offenders or suppressing material evidence of the commission of such offence, the State Government may, by notification in the Official Gazette, impose a collective fine on such inhabitants and apportion such fine amongst the inhabitants who are liable collectively to pay it, and such apportionment shall be made according to the State Government's judgement of the respective means of such inhabitants and in making any such apportionment the State Government may assign a portion of such fine to a Hindu undivided family to be payable by it;

Provided that the fine apportioned to an inhabitant shall not be realised until the petition, if any, filed by him under sub-section (3) is disposed of.

(2) The notification made under sub-section (1) shall be proclaimed in the area by beat of drum or in such other manner as the State Government may think best in the circumstances to bring the imposition of the collective fine to the notice of the inhabitants of the said area.

(3a) Any person aggrieved by the imposition of the collective fine under sub-section (1) or by the order of apportionment, may, within the prescribed period, file a petition before the State Government or such other authority as that Government may specify in this behalf for being exempted from such fine or for modification of the order of apportionment:

---

30. Ins. by s. 13, *ibid.*, (w.e.f. 19-11-1976).

Provided that no fee shall be charged for filing such petition.

(b) The State Government or the authority specified by it shall, after giving to the petitioner a reasonable opportunity of being heard, pass such order as it may think fit :

Provided that the amount of the fine exempted or reduced under this section shall not be realisable from any person, and the total fine imposed on the inhabitants or an area under sub-section (*1*) shall be deemed to have been reduced to that extent.

(4) Notwithstanding anything contained in sub-section (3), the State Government may exempt the victims of any offence punishable under this Act or any person who does not, in its opinion, fall within the category of persons specified in sub-section (1), from the liability to pay the collective fine imposed under sub-section (1) or any portion thereof.

(*5*) The portion of collective fine payable by any person (including a Hindu undivided family) may be recovered in the manner provided by the Code of Criminal Procedure, 1973, for the recovery of fines imposed by a Court as if such portion were a fine imposed by a Magistrate.

11. Enhanced Penalty on Subsequent Conviction

Whoever having already been convicted of an offence under this Act or of an abetment of such offence is again convicted of any such offence or abetment, [31][shall, on conviction, be punishable–

(a) for the second offence, with imprisonment for a term of not less than six months and not more than one year, and also with fine which shall not be less than two hundred rupees and not more than five hundred rupees;

---

31. Subs. by Act 106 of 1976, s. 14, for certain words (w.e.f. 19-11-1976).

(b) for the third offence or any offence subsequent to the third offence, with imprisonment for a term of not less than one year and not more than two years, and also with fine which shall be not less than five hundred rupees and not more than one thousand rupees].

12. Presumption by Courts in Certain Cases

Where any act constituting an offence under this Act is committed in relation to a member of a Scheduled Caste [32]* * *, the court shall presume, unless the contrary is proved, that such act was committed on the ground of "untouchability".

13. Limitation of Jurisdiction of Civil Courts

(1) No Civil Court shall entertain or continue any suit or proceeding or shall pass any decree or order or execute wholly or partially any decree or order if the claim involved in such suit or proceeding or if the passing of such decree or order or if such execution would in any way be contrary to the provisions of this Act,

(2) No court shall, in adjudicating any matter or executing any decree or order, recognise any custom or usage imposing any disability on any person on the ground of "untouchability".

14 Offences by Companies

(1) If the person committing an offence under this Act is a company, every person who at the time the offence was committed was a charge of, and was responsible to, the company for the business of the company, shall be deemed to be guilty of the offence and shall be liable to be proceeded against and punished accordingly :

Provided that nothing contained in this sub-section shall render any such person liable to any punishment, if he proves that the offence

---

32. The words "as defined in clause (2A) of article 366 of Constitution" omitted by s. 15, *ibid.*, (w.e.f. 19-11-1976).

was committed without his knowledge or that he exercised all due diligence to prevent the commission of such offence.

(2) Notwithstanding anything contained in subsection (1), where an offence under this Act has been committed with the consent of any director or manager, secretary or other officer of the company, such director, manager, secretary or other officer shall also be deemed to be guilty of that offence and shall be liable to be proceeded against and punished accordingly.

Explanation– For the purposes of this section.–

(a) "company" means any body corporate and includes a firm or other association of individuals; and
(b) "director" in relation to a firm means a partner in the firm.

[33][**14A. Protection of Action taken in Good Faith**

(1) No suit, prosecution or other legal proceeding, shall lie against the Central Government or a State Government for anything which is in good faith done or intended to be done under this Act.

(2) No suit, prosecution or other legal proceeding shall lie against the Central Government or a State Government for any damage caused or likely to be caused by anything which is in good faith done or intended to be done under this Act.]

[34][**15 Offences to be Cognizable and Triable Summarily**

(1) Notwithstanding anything contained in Code of Criminal Procedure, 1973, (2 of 1974) every offence punishable under this Act shall be cognizable and every such offence, except where it is punishable with imprisonment for a minimum

---

33. Ins. by Act 106 of 1976, s. 16(w.e.f. 19-11-1976).
34. Subs, by s. 17, *ibid.*, for s. 15 (w.e.f. 19-11-1976)

term exceeding three months may be tried summarily by a Judicial Magistrate of the first class or in a metropolitan area by a Metropolitan Magistrate in accordance with the procedure specified in the said Code.

(2) Notwithstanding anything contained in Code of Criminal Procedure, 1973, (2 of 1974) when any public servant is alleged to have committed the offence of abetment of an offence punishable under this Act, while acting or purporting to act in the discharge of his official duty, no court shall take cognizance of such offence of abetment except with the previous sanction–

(a) of the Central Government, in the case of a person employed in connection with the affairs of the Union; and

(b) of the State Government, in the case of a person employed in connection with the affairs of a State;

15A. Duty of State Government to Ensure that the Rights Accruing from the Abolition of "Untouchability" may be Availed of by the Concerned Persons

(1) Subject to such rules as the Central Government may make in this behalf, the State Government shall take such measures as may be necessary for ensuring that the rights arising from the abolition of "untouchability" are made available to, and are availed of by, the person subjected to any disability arising out of "untouchability".

(2) In particular, and without prejudice to the generality of the provisions of sub-section (1), such measures may include –

(i) the provision of adequate faciiities, including legal aid, to the persons subjected to any disability arising out of "untouchability" to enable them to avail themselves of such rights;

(ii) the appointment of officers for initiating or exercising supervision over prosecutions for the contravention of the provisions of this Act;

(iii) the setting up of special courts for the trial of offences under this Act;

(iv) the setting up of Committees as such appropriate levels as the State Government may think fit to assist the State Government in formulating or implementing such measures;

(v) provision for a periodic survey of the working of the provisions of this Act with a view to suggesting measures for the better implementation of the provisions of this Act;

(vi) the identification of the areas where persons are under any disability arising out of "untouchability" and adoption of such measures as would ensure the removal of such disability from such areas;

(3) The Central Government shall take such steps as may be necessary to co-ordinate the measures taken by the State Government under sub-section (1).

(4) The Central Government shall, every year, place on the Table of each House of Parliament, a report on the measures taken by itself and by the State Governments in pursuance of the provisions of this section.

16. Act to Override Other Laws

Save as otherwise expressly provided in this Act, the provisions of this Act shall have effect notwithstanding anything inconsistent therewith contained in any other law for the time being in force, or any custom or usage or any instrument having effect by virtue of any such law or any decree or order of any court or other authority.

[35][**16A. Probation of Offenders Act, 1958 not to Apply to Persons above the Age of fourteen years**

The provisions of the Probation of Offenders Act, 1958, (20 of 1958) shall not apply to any person above the age of fourteen

---

35. Ins. by Act. 106 of 1976, s. 18 (w.e.f. 19-11-1976).

years who is found guilty of having committed any offence punishable under this Act.

16B. Power to Make Rules

(1) The Central Government may, by notification in the Official Gazette, make rules to carry out the provisions of this Act.

(2) Every rule made by the Central Government under this Act shall be laid, as soon as may be after it is made, before each House of Parliament while it is in session for a total period of thirty days which may be comprised in one session or in two or more successive sessions, and if, before the expiry of the session immediately following the session or the successive sessions aforesaid, both Houses agree in making any modification in the rule or both Houses agree that the rule should not be made, the rule shall thereafter have effect only in such modified form or be of no effect, as the case may be; so, however, that any such modification or annulment shall be without prejudice to the validity of anything previously done under that rule.

17. Repeal

The enactments specified in the Schedule are hereby repealed to the extent to which they or any of the provisions contained therein correspond or are repugnant to this Act of to any of the provisions contained therein.

THE SCHEDULE

(*See* Section 17)

1. The Bihar Harijan (Removal of Civil Disabilities) Act, 1949 (Bihar Act XIX of 1949).
2. The Bombay Harijan (Removal of Social Disabilities) Act, 1946 (Bombay Act X of 1947).

3. The Bombay Harijan Temple Entry Act, 1947 (Bombay Act XXXV of 1947).
4. The Central Provinces and Berar Scheduled Castes (Removal of Civil Disabilities) Act, 1947 (Central Provinces and Berar Act XXIV of 1947).
5. The Central Provinces and Berar Temple Entry Authorisation Act, 1947 (Central Provinces and Berar Act XLI of 1947).
6. The East Punjab (Removal of Religious and Social Disabilities) Act, 1948 (East Punjab Act XVI of 1948).
7. The Madras Removal of Civil Disabilities Act, 1938 (Madras Act XXI of 1938).
8. The Orissa Removal of Civil Disabilities Act, 1946 (Orissa Act XI of 1946).
9. The Orissa Temple Entry Authorisation Act, 1948 (Orissa Act XI of 1948).
10. The United Provinces Removal of Social Disabilities Act, 1947 (U.P. Act XIV of 1947).
11. The West Bengal Hindu Social Disabilities Removal Act, 1948 (West Bengal Act XXXVII of 1948).
12. The Hyderabad Harijan Temple Entry Regulations, 1358F (No LV of 1358 Fasli).
13. The Hyderabad Harijan (Removal of Social Disabilities) Regulation, 1358F (No LVI of 1358 Fasli).
14. The Madhya Bharat Harijan Ayogta Nivaran Vidhan, Samvat 2005 (Madhya Bharat Act No. 15 of 1949).
15. The Removal of Civil Disabilities Act, 1943 (Mysore Act XLII of 1943).
16. The Mysore Temple Entry Authorisation Act, 1948 (Mysore Act XIV of 1948).
17. The Saurashtra Harijan (Removal of Social Disabilities) Ordinance (No XL of 1948).
18. The Travancore-Cochin Removal of Social Disabilities Act, 1125 (Travancore-Cochin Act VIII of 1125).

19. The Travancore-Cochin Temple Entry, Removal of DisabilitiesAct, 1950 (Travancore-Cochin Act XXVII of 1950).
20. The Coorg Scheduled Castes (Removal of Civil and Social Disabilities) Act, 1949 (Coorg Act I of 1949).
21. The Coorg Temple Entry Authorisation Act, 1949 (Coorg Act II of 1949).

APPENDIX-II

The Scheduled Castes and the Scheduled Tribes (Prevention of Atrocities) Act, 1989

No. 33 of 1989

[11th September, 1989]

An Act to prevent the commission of offences of atrocities against the members of the Scheduled Castes and the Scheduled Tribes, to provide for Special Courts for the trial of such offences and for the relief and rehabilitation of the victims of such offences and for matters connected therewith or incidental thereto.

BE it enacted by Parliament in the Fortieth Year of the Republic of India as follows:

CHAPTER I
PRELIMINARY

1. Short title, extent and commencement

(1) This Act may be called the Scheduled Castes and the Scheduled Tribes (Prevention of Atrocities) Act, 1989.
(2) It extends to the whole of India except the State of Jammu and Kashmir.
(3) It shall come into force on such date as the Central Government may, by notification in the Official Gazette, appoint.

2. Definitions

(1) In this Act, unless the context otherwise requires,—

(a) "atrocity" means an offence punishable under section 3;

(b) "Code" means the Code of Criminal Procedure, 1973 (2 of 1974);

(c) "Scheduled Castes and Scheduled Tribes" shall have the meanings assigned to them respectively under clause (24) and clause (25) of article 366 of the Constitution;

(d) "Special Courts" means a Court of Session specified as a Special Court in Section 14;

(e) "Special Public Prosecutor" means a Public Prosecutor specified as a Special Public Prosecutor or an advocate referred to in Section 15;

(f) words and expressions used but not defined in this Act and defined in the Code or in the Indian Penal Code (45 of 1860) shall have the meanings assigned to them respectively in the Code, or as the case may be, in the Indian Penal Code.

(2) Any reference in this Act to any enactment or any provision thereof shall, in relation to an area in which such enactment or such provision is not in force, be construed as a reference to the corresponding law, if any, in force in that area.

CHAPTER II
OFFENCES OF ATROCITIES

3. Punishment for offences of atrocities

(1) Whoever, not being a member or a Scheduled Caste or a Scheduled Tribe,–

(i) forces a member of a Scheduled Caste or a Scheduled Tribe to drink or eat any inedible or obnoxious substance;

(ii) acts with intent to cause injury, insult or annoyance to any member of Scheduled Caste or a Scheduled Tribe by dumping excreta, waste matter, carcasses or any other obnoxious substance in his premises or neighbourhood;

(iii) forcibly removes clothes from the person of a member of Scheduled Caste or a Scheduled Tribe or parades him naked or with painted face or body or commits any similar act which is derogatory to human dignity;

(iv) wrongfully occupies or cultivates any land owned by, or allotted to, or notified by any competent authority to be allotted to, a member of Scheduled Caste or a Scheduled Tribe or gets the land allotted to him transferred;

(v) wrongfully dispossesses a member of Scheduled Caste or a Scheduled Tribe from his land or premises or interferes with the enjoyment of his rights over any land, premises or water;

(vi) compels or entices a member of Scheduled Caste or a Scheduled Tribe to do 'begar' or other similar forms of forced or bonded labour other than any compulsory service for public purposes imposed by Government;

(vii) forces or intimidates a member of Scheduled Caste or a Scheduled Tribe not to vote or vote to a particular candidate or to vote in a manner other than that provided by law;

(viii) institutes false, malicious or vexatious suit or criminal or other legal proceedings against a member of Scheduled Caste or a Scheduled Tribe;

(ix) gives any false or frivolous information to any public servant and thereby cause such public servant to use his lawful power to the injury or annoyance of a member of a Scheduled Caste or a Scheduled Tribe;

(x) intentionally insults or intimidates with intent to humiliate a member of Scheduled Caste or a Scheduled Tribe in any place within public view;

(xi) assaults or uses force to any woman belonging to Scheduled Caste or a Scheduled Tribe with intent to dishonour or outrage her modesty;

(xii) being in a position to dominate the will of a woman belonging to a Scheduled Caste or a Scheduled Tribe and uses that position to exploit her sexually to which she would not have otherwise agreed;

(xiii) corrupts or fouls the water of any spring, reservoir or any other source ordinarily used by members of Scheduled Caste or a Scheduled Tribe so as to render it less fit for the purpose for which it is ordinarily used;

(xiv) denies a member of Scheduled Caste or a Scheduled Tribe any customary right of passage to a place of public resort or obstructs such member so as to prevent him from using or having access to a place of public resort to which other members of public or any section thereof have a right to use or access to; and

(xv) forces or causes a member of a Scheduled Caste or a Scheduled Tribe to leave his house, village or other place of residence;

shall be punishable with imprisonment for a term which shall not be less than six months but which may extend to five years and with fine.

(2) Whoever, not being a member of Scheduled Caste or a Scheduled Tribe,—

(i) gives or fabricates false evidence intending thereby to cause, or knowing it to be likely that he will thereby cause, any member of a Scheduled Caste or a Scheduled Tribe to be convicted of an offence which is capital by the law for the time being in force shall be punished with imprisonment for life and with fine; and if an innocent member of Scheduled Caste or a Scheduled Tribe be convicted and executed in consequence of such false or fabricated evidence, the person who gives or fabricates such false evidence, shall be punished with death;

(ii) gives or fabricates false evidence intending thereby to cause, or knowing it to be likely that he will thereby cause, any member of Scheduled Caste or a Scheduled Tribe to be convicted of an offence which is not capital but punishable with imprisonment for a term of seven years or upwards, shall be punishable with imprisonment for a term which shall not be less than six months but which may extend to seven years or upwards and with fine;

(iii) commits mischief by fire or any explosive substance intending to cause or knowing it to be likely that he will thereby cause damage to any property belonging to a member of a Scheduled Caste or a Scheduled Tribe, shall be punishable with imprisonment for a term which shall not be less than six months but which may extend to seven years and with fine;

(iv) commits mischief by the fire or any explosive substance intending to cause or knowing it to be likely that he will thereby cause destruction of any building which is ordinarily used as a place of worship or as a place for human dwelling or as a place for custody of the property by a member of a Scheduled Caste or a Scheduled Tribe, shall be punishable with imprisonment for life and with fine;

(v) commits any offence under the Indian Penal Code (45 of 1860) punishable with imprisonment for a term of ten years or more against a person or property on the ground that such person is a member of a Scheduled Caste or a Scheduled Tribe or such property belongs to such member, shall be punishable with imprisonment for life and with fine;

(vi) knowingly or having reason to believe that an offence has been committed under this Chapter, causes any evidence of the commission of that offence to disappear with the intention of screening the offender from legal punishment, or with that intention gives any information respecting the offence which he knows or believes to be false, shall be punishable with the punishment provided for that offence; or

(vii) being a public servant, commits any offence under this section, shall be punishable with imprisonment for a term which shall not be less than one year but which may extend to the punishment provided for that offence.

4. Punishment for neglect of duties — Whoever, being a public servant but not being a member of a Scheduled Caste or a Scheduled Tribe, wilfully neglects his duties required to be performed by him under this Act, shall be punishable with imprisonment for a term which shall not be less than six months but which may extend to one year.

5. Enhanced punishment for subsequent conviction — Whoever, having already been convicted of an offence under this Chapter is convicted for the second offence or any offence subsequent to the second offence, shall be punishable with imprisonment for a term which shall not be less than one year but which may extend to the punishment provided for that offence.

6. Application of certain provisions of the Indian Penal Code — Subject to the other provisions of this Act, the provisions of Section 34, Chapter III, Chapter IV, Chapter V, Chapter VA, Section 149 and Chapter XXIII of the Indian Penal Code (45 of 1860), shall, so far as may be, apply for the purposes of this Act as they apply for the purposes of the Indian Penal Code.

7. Forfeiture of property of certain persons

(1) Where a person has been convicted of any offence punishable under this Chapter, the Special Court may, in addition to awarding any punishment, by order in writing, declare that any property, movable or immovable or both, belonging to the person, which has been used for the commission of that offence, shall stand forfeited to Government.

(2) Where any person is accused of any offence under this Chapter, it will be open to the Special Court trying him to pass an order that all or any of the properties, movable or immovable or both, belonging to him, shall, during in the period of such trial, be attached, and where such trial ends in conviction, the property so attached shall be liable to forfeiture to the extent as required for the purpose of realisation of any fine imposed under this Chapter.

8. Presumption as to offences – In a prosecution under this Chapter, if it is proved that –

(a) the accused rendered any financial assistance to the person accused of, or reasonably suspected of, committing an offence under this Chapter, the Special Court shall presume, unless the contrary is proved, that such person had abetted the offence;

(b) a group of persons committed an offence under this Chapter and if it is proved that the offence committed was a sequel to any existing dispute regarding land or any other matter, it shall be presumed that the offence was committed in furtherance of the common intention or in prosecution of the common object.

9. Conferment of Powers

(1) Notwithstanding anything contained in the Code or in any other provision of this Act, the State Government may, if it considers it necessary or expedient so to do, –

(a) for the prevention of and for coping with any offence under this Act, or

(b) for any case or class or group of cases under this Act, in any district or part thereof, confer, by notification in the Official Gazette, on any officer of the State Government, the powers exercisable by a police officer under the Code in such district or part thereof or, as the case may be, for such case or class or group of cases, and in particular, the powers of arrest, investigation and prosecution of persons before any Special Court.

(2) All officers of police and all other officers of Government shall assist the officer referred to in sub-section (1) in the execution of the provisions of this Act or any rule, scheme or order made thereunder.

(3) The provisions of the Code shall, so far as may, apply to the exercise of the powers by an officer under sub-section (1).

CHAPTER III
EXTERNMENT

10. Removal of person likely to commit offence

(1) Where the Special Court is satisfied, upon a complaint or a police report that a person is likely to commit an offence under Chapter II of this Act in any area included in the 'Scheduled Areas' or 'Tribal Areas' as referred to in Article 244 of the Constitution, it may, by order in writing, direct such person to remove himself beyond the limits of such area, by such route and within such time as may be specified in the order, and not to return to that area from which he was directed to remove himself for such period, not exceeding two years, as may be specified in the order.

(2) The Special Court shall, along with the order under sub-section (1), communicate to the person directed under the sub-section the grounds on which such order has been made.

(3) The Special Court may revoke or modify the order made under sub-section (1), for the reasons to be recorded in writing, on the representation made by the person against whom such order has been made or any other person on his behalf within thirty days from the date of the order.

11. Procedure on failure of person to remove himself from an area and enter thereon after removal –

(1) If a person to whom a direction has been issued under section 10 to remove himself from any area –

(a) fails to remove himself as directed; or
(b) having so removed himself enters such area within the period specified in the order,

otherwise than with the permission in writing of the Special Court under sub-section (2), the Special Court may cause him to be arrested and removed by police custody to such place outside such area as the Special Court may specify.

(2) The Special Court may, by order in writing, permit any person in respect of whom an order under section 10 has been made, to return to the area from which he was directed to remove himself for such temporary period and subject to such conditions as may be specified in such order and may require him to execute a bond with or without surety for the due servation of the conditions imposed.

(3) The Special Court may at any time revoke any such permission.

(4) Any person, who with such permission, returns to the area from which he was directed to remove himself, shall observe the conditions imposed, and at the expiry of the temporary period for which he was permitted to return, or on the revocation of such permission before the expiry of such temporary period, shall remove himself outside such area and shall not return thereto within the unexpired portion specified under section 10 without a fresh permission.

(5) If a person fails to observe any of the conditions imposed or to remove himself accordingly or having so removed himself enters or returns to such area without fresh permission, the Special Court may cause him to be arrested and removed in police custody to such place outside such area as the Special Court may specify.

12. **Taking measurements and photographs, etc., of persons against whom order under section 10 is made –**

(1) Every person against whom an order has been made under section 10 shall, if so required by the Special Court, allow his measurements and photographs to be taken by a police officer.

(2) If any person referred to in sub-section (1), when required to allow his measurements or photographs to be taken, resists or refuses to allow the taking of such measurements or photographs, it shall be lawful to use all necessary means to secure the taking thereof.

(3) Resistance to or refusal to allow the taking of measurements or photographs under sub-section (2) shall be deemed to be an offence under section 186 of the Indian Penal Code (*45 of 1860*).

(4) Where an order under section 10 is revoked, all measurements and photographs (including negatives) taken under sub-section (2) shall be destroyed or made over to the person against whom such order is made.

13. Penalty for non-compliance of order under Section 10 –

Any person contravening an order of the Special Court made under Section 10 shall be punishable with imprisonment for a term which may extend to one year and with fine.

CHAPTER IV
SPECIAL COURTS

14. **Special Court** – For the purpose of providing for speedy trial, the State Government shall, with the concurrence of the Chief Justice of the High Court, by notification in the Official Gazette, specify for each district a Court of Session to be a Special Court to try the offences under this Act.

15. **Special Public Prosecutor** – For every Special Court, the State Government shall, by notification in the Official Gazette, specify a Public Prosecutor or appoint an advocate who has been in practice as an advocate for not less than seven years, as a Special Public Prosecutor for the purpose of conducting cases in that Court.

CHAPTER V
MISCELLANEOUS

16. **Power of State Government to impose collective fine** – The provisions of Section 10A of the Protection of Civil Rights Act, 1955 (22 of 1955) shall, so far as may be, apply for the purposes of imposition and realisation of collective fine and for all other matters connected therewith under this Act.

17. **Preventive action to be taken by the law and order machinery** – (1) A District Magistrate or Sub-divisional Magistrate or any other Executive Magistrate or any police officer not below the rank of Deputy Superintendent of Police may, on receiving information and after such inquiry as he may think necessary, has reason to believe that a person or group of persons not belonging to the Scheduled Castes or the Scheduled Tribes, residing in or frequenting any place within the local limits of his jurisdiction is likely to commit an offence or has threatened to commit any offence under this Act and is of the opinion that there is sufficient ground for proceeding, declare such an area to be an area prone to atrocities and take necessary action for keeping the peace and good behaviour and maintenance of public order and tranquillity and may take preventive action.

(2) The provisions of Chapters VIII, X and XI of the Code shall, so far as may be, apply for the purposes of sub-section (1).

(3) The State Government may, by notification in the Official Gazette, make one or more scheme specifying the matter in which the officers referred to in sub-section (1) shall take appropriate action specified in such scheme or schemes to prevent atrocities and to restore the feeling of security amongst the members of the Scheduled Castes and the Scheduled Tribes.

18. Section 438 of the Code not to apply to persons committing an offence under the Act – Nothing in Section 438 of the Code shall apply in relation to any case involving the arrest of any person on an accusation of having committed an offence under this Act.

19. Section 360 of the Code or the provisions of the Probation of Offenders Act not to apply to persons guilty of an offence under the Act – The provisions of Section 360 of the Code and the provisions of the Probation of Offenders Act, 1958 (20 of 1958) shall not apply to any person above the age of eighteen years who is found guilty of having committed an offence under this Act.

20. Act to override other laws – Save as otherwise provided in this Act, the provision of this Act shall have effect notwithstanding anything inconsistent therewith contained in any other law for the time being in force or any custom or usage or any instrument having effect by virtue of any such law.

21. Duty of Government to ensure effective implementation of the Act –

(1) Subject to such rules as the Central Government may make in this behalf, the State Government shall take such measures as may be necessary for the implementation of this Act.

(2) In particular, and without prejudice to the generality of the foregoing provisions, such measures may include,–

(i) the provision for adequate facilities, including legal aid, to the persons subjected to atrocities to enable them to avail themselves of justice;

(ii) the provision for travelling and maintenance expenses to witnesses, including the victims of atrocities, during investigation and trial of offences under this Act;

(iii) the provision for the economic and social rehabilitation of the victims of the atrocities;

(iv) the appointment of officers for initiating or exercising supervision over prosecutions for the contravention of the provisions of this Act;

(v) the setting up of committee at such appropriate levels as the State Government may think fit as to assist that Government in formulation or implementation of such measures;

(vi) provision for a periodic survey of the working of the provisions of this Act with a view to suggesting measures for the better implementation of the provisions of this Act; and

(vii) the identification of the areas where the members of the Scheduled Castes and the Scheduled Tribes are likely to be subjected to atrocities and adoption of such measures as to ensure safety for such members.

(3) The Central Government shall take such steps as may be necessary to co-ordinate the measures taken by the State Government under sub-section (1).

(4) The Central Government shall, every year, place on the table of each House of Parliament a report on the measures taken by itself and by the State Governments in pursuance of the provisions of this section.

22. Protection of action taken in good faith – No suit, prosecution or other legal proceedings shall lie against the Central Government or against the State Government or any officer or authority of Government or any other person for anything which is in good faith done or intended to be done under this Act.

23. Power to make rules –

(1) The Central Government may, by notification in the Official Gazette, make rules for carrying out the purposes of this Act.

(2) Every rule made under this Act shall be laid, as soon as may be after it is made, before each House of Parliament, while it is in session for a total period of thirty days which may be comprised in one session or in two or more successive sessions, and if, before the expiry of the session immediately following the session or the successive sessions aforesaid, both Houses agree making any modification in the rule or both Houses agree that the rule should not be made, the rule shall thereafter have effect only in such modified form or be of no effect, as the case may be; so, however that any such modification or annulment shall be without prejudice to the validity of anything previously done under that rule.

THE SCHEDULED CASTES AND THE SCHEDULED TRIBES (PREVENTION OF ATROCITIES) RULES, 1995*

In exercise of the powers conferred by sub-section (1) of section 23 of the Scheduled Castes and the Scheduled Tribes (Prevention of Atrocities) Act, 1989 (33 of 1989), the Central Government hereby makes the following rules, namely:

1. **Short title and commencement –**

(1) These rules may be called the Scheduled Castes and the Scheduled Tribes (Prevention of Atrocities) Rules, 1995.
(2) They shall come into force on the date of their publication in the Official Gazette.

2. **Definitions** – In the rules, unless the context otherwise requires:–
   (a) "Act" means the Scheduled Castes and the Scheduled Tribes (Prevention of Atrocities) Act, 1989 (33 of 1989);
   (b) "dependent" with its grammatical variations and cognate expressions includes *wife, children*, whether married or unmarried, dependent parents, widowed sister, widow and children of pre-deceased son of a victim of atrocity;
   (c) "identified area" means such area where State Government has reason to believe that atrocity may take place or there is an apprehension of reoccurrence of an offence under the Act or an area prone to victim of atrocity;
   (d) "Non-Government Organisation" means a voluntary organisation engaged in the welfare activities relating to the Scheduled Castes and the Scheduled Tribes and

---

* *Vide* G.S.R. 316(E), dated 31st March, 1995, published in the Gazette of India, Extra., Pt. II, Sec. 3(i), dated 31st March, 1995.

registered under the Societies Registration Act, 1866 (21 of 1960) or under any law for the registration of documents or such organisation for the time being in force;

(e) "Schedule" means the Schedule annexed to these rules;
(f) "Section" means section of the Act;
(g) "State Government" in relation to a Union Territory, means the Administrator of that Union Territory appointed by the President under Article 239 of the Constitution;
(h) words and expressions used herein and not defined but defined in the Act shall have the meanings respectively assigned to them in the Act.

3. **Precautionary and Preventive Measures** – With a view to prevent atrocities on the Scheduled Castes and Scheduled Tribes, the State Government shall:-

(i) identify the area where it has reason to believe that atrocity may take place or there is an apprehension of reoccurrence of an offence under the Act;
(ii) order the District Magistrate and Superintendent of Police or any other officer to visit the identified area and review the law and order situation;
(iii) if deem necessary, in the identified area cancel the arms licences of the persons, not being member of the Scheduled Castes and Scheduled Tribes, their near relations, servants or employees and family friends and get such arms deposited in the Government Armoury;
(iv) seize all illegal fire arms and prohibit any illegal manufacture of fire arms;
(v) with a view to ensure the safety of person and property, if deem necessary, provide arms licences to the members of the Scheduled Castes and Scheduled Tribes;
(vi) constitute a high power State-level committee, district and divisional level committees or such number of other committees as deem proper and necessary for

assisting the Government in implementation of the provisions of the Act;

(vii) set-up a vigilance and monitoring committee to suggest effective measures to implement the provisions of the Act;

(viii) set-up Awareness centres and organise Workshops in the identified area or at some other place to educate the persons belonging to the Scheduled Castes and the Scheduled Tribes about their rights and the protection available to them under the provisions of various Central and State enactments or rules, regulations and schemes framed thereunder;

(ix) encourage Non-Government Organisations for establishing and maintaining Awareness Centres and organising workshops and provide them necessary financial and other sort of assistance;

(x) deploy special police force in the identified area;

(xi) by the end of every quarter, review the law and order situation, functioning of different committees, performance of Special Public Prosecutors, Investigating Officers and other Officers responsible for implementing the provisions of the Act and the cases registered under the Act.

4. Supervision of Prosecution and Submission of Report –

(1) The State Government on the recommendation of the District Magistrate shall prepare for each District a panel of such number of eminent senior advocates who have been in practice for not less than seven years, as it may deem necessary for conducting cases in the Special Courts. Similarly, in consultation with the Director of Prosecution/ in-charge of the prosecution, a panel of such number of Public Prosecutors as it may deem necessary for conducting cases in the Special Courts, shall also be specified. Both

these panels shall be notified in the Official Gazette of the State and shall remain in force for a period of three years.

(2) The District Magistrate and the Director of Prosecution/in-charge of the prosecution shall review at least twice in a calendar year, in the month of January and July, the performance of Special Public Prosecutors so specified or appointed and submit a report to the State Government.

(3) If the State Government is satisfied or has reason to believe that a Special Public Prosecutor so appointed or specified has not conducted the case to the best of the ability and with due care and caution, his name may be, for the reasons to be recorded in writing, denotified.

(4) The District Magistrate and the officer-in-charge of the prosecution at the District level, shall review the position of cases registered under the Act and submit a monthly report on or before 20th day of each subsequent month to the Director of Prosecution and the State Government. This report shall specify the actions taken/proposed to be taken in respect of investigation and prosecution of each case.

(5) Notwithstanding anything contained in sub-rule (1) the District Magistrate or the Sub-Divisional Magistrate may, if deem necessary or if so desired by the victims of atrocity engage an eminent Senior Advocate for conducting cases in the Special Courts on such payment of fee as he may consider appropriate.

(6) Payment of fee to the Special Public Prosecutor shall be fixed by the State Government on a scale higher than the other panel advocates in the State.

5. Information to Police Officer in-charge of a Police Station–

(1) Every information relating to the commission of an offence under the Act, if given orally to an officer in-charge of a police station shall be reduced to writing by him or under his direction, and be read over to the informant, and every such information, whether given in writing or reduced to

writing as aforesaid, shall be signed by the persons giving it, and the substance thereof shall be entered in a book to be maintained by that police station.

(2) A copy of the information as so recorded under sub-rule (1) above shall be given forthwith, free of cost, to the informant.

(3) Any person aggrieved by a refusal on the part of an officer in-charge of a police station to record the information referred to in sub-rule (1) may send the substance of such information, in writing and by post, to the Superintendent of Police concerned who after investigation either by himself or by a police officer not below the rank of Deputy Superintendent of Police, shall make an order in writing to the officer in-charge of the concerned police station to enter the substance of that information to be entered in the book to be maintained by the police station.

6. Spot inspection by officers –

(1) Whenever the District Magistrate or the Sub-Divisional Magistrate or any other Executive Magistrate or any police officer not below the rank of Deputy Superintendent of Police receives an information from any person or upon his own knowledge that an atrocity has been committed on the members of the Scheduled Castes or the Scheduled Tribes within his jurisdiction, he shall immediately himself visit the place of occurrence to assess the extent of atrocity, loss of life, loss and damage to the property and submit a report forthwith to the State Government.

(2) The District Magistrate or the Sub-Divisional Magistrate or any other Executive Magistrate and the Superintendent of Police/Deputy Superintendent of Policc aftcr inspecting the place or area shall on the spot–

(i) draw a list of victims, their family members and dependents entitled for relief;

(ii) prepare a detailed report of the extent of atrocity loss and damage to the property of the victims;

(iii) order for intensive police patrolling in the area;

(iv) take effective and necessary steps to provide protection to the witnesses and other sympathisers of the victims;

(v) provide immediate relief to the victims.

7. Investigating Officer–

(1) An offence committed under the Act shall be investigated by a police officer not below the rank of a Deputy Superintendent of Police. The investigating officer shall be appointed by the State Government/Director General of Police/Superintendent of Police after taking into account his past experience, sense of ability and justice to perceive the implication of the case and investigate it alongwith right lines within the shortest possible time.

(2) The investigating officer so appointed under sub-rule (1) shall complete the investigation on top priority within thirty days and submit the report to the Superintendent of Police who in turn will immediately forward the report to the Director General of Police of the State Government.

(3) The Home Secretary and the Social Welfare Secretary to the State Government, Director of Prosecution/the officer in-charge of Prosecution and the Director General of Police shall review by the end of every quarter the position of all investigations done by the investigating officer.

8. Setting up of the Scheduled Castes and the Scheduled Tribes Protection Cell –

(1) The State Government shall set up the Scheduled Caste and the Scheduled Tribes Protection Cell at the State headquarters under the charge of Director of Police/Inspector General of Police. This Cell shall be responsible for –

(i) conducting survey of the identified area;

(ii) maintaining public order and tranquillity in the identified area;

(iii) recommending to the State Government for deployment of special police force or establishment of special police post in the identified area;

(iv) making investigations about the probable causes leading to an offence under the Act;

(v) restoring the feeling of security amongst the members of the Scheduled Castes and the Scheduled Tribes;

(vi) informing the nodal officer and special officer about the law and order situation in the identified area;

(vii) making enquiries about the investigation and spot inspections conducted by various officers;

(viii) making enquiries about the action taken by the Superintendent of Police in the cases where an officer in-charge of the police station has refused to enter an information in a book to be maintained by that police-station under sub-rule (3) of rule 5;

(ix) making enquiries about the wilful negligence by a public servant;

(x) reviewing the position of cases registered under the Act; and

(xi) submitting a monthly report on or before 20th day of each subsequent month to the State Government/nodal officer about the action taken/proposed to be taken in respect of the above.

9. **Nomination of Nodal Officer** – The Sate Government shall nominate a nodal officer of the level of a Secretary to the State Government preferably belonging to the Scheduled Castes or the Scheduled Tribes, for co-ordinating the functioning of the District Magistrate and Superintendent of Police or other officers authorised by them, investigating officers and other officers responsible for implementing the provisions of the Act. By the end of the every quarter, the nodal officer shall review–

(i) the reports received by the State Government under

sub-rule (2) and (4) of rule 4, rule 6, clause (xi) of rule 8;

(ii) the position of cases registered under the Act;

(iii) law and order situation in the identified area;

(iv) various kinds of measures adopted for providing immediate relief in cash or kind or both to the victims of atrocity or his or her dependents;

(v) adequacy of immediate facilities like rationing, clothing, shelter, legal aid, travelling allowance, daily allowance and transport facilities provided to the victims of atrocity or his/her dependents;

(vi) performance of Non-Governmental Organisations, the Scheduled Castes and the Scheduled Tribes Protection Cell, various committees and the public servants responsible for implementing the provisions of the Act.

10. Appointment of a Special Officer – In the identified area a Special Officer not below the rank of a Additional District Magistrate shall be appointed to coordinate with the District Magistrate, Superintendent of Police or other officers responsible for implementing the provisions of the Act, various committees and the Scheduled Castes and the Scheduled Tribes Protection Cell.

The Special Officer shall be responsible for –

(i) providing immediate relief and other facilities to the victims of atrocity and initiate necessary measures to prevent or avoid re-occurrence of atrocity;

(ii) setting up an awareness centre and organising workshop in the identified area or at the district headquarters to educate the persons belonging to the Scheduled Castes and the Scheduled Tribes about their rights and the protection available to them under the provisions of various Central and State enactments or rules and schemes etc. framed therein;

(iii) co-ordinating with the Non-Governmental Organisation and providing necessary facilities and financial and other type of assistance to Non-Governmental Organisations for maintaining centres or organising workshops.

11. Travelling allowance, daily allowance, maintenance expenses and transport facilities to the victim of atrocity, his or her dependent and witnesses –

(1) Every victim of atrocity or his/her dependent and witnesses shall be paid to and fro rail fare by second class in express/mail/passenger train or actual bus or taxi fare from his/her place of residence or place of stay to the place of investigation or hearing of trial of an offence under the Act.

(2) The District Magistrate or the Sub-Divisional Magistrate or any other Executive Magistrate shall make necessary arrangements for providing transport facilities or reimbursement of full payment thereof to the victims of atrocity and witnesses for visiting the investigating officer, Superintendent of Police/Deputy Superintendent of Police, District Magistrate or any other Executive Magistrate.

(3) Every woman witness, the victim of atrocity or her dependent being a woman or a minor, a person more than sixty years of age and a person having 40 per cent or more disability shall be entitled to be accompanied by an attendant of her/his choice. The attendant shall also be paid travelling and maintenance expenses as applicable to the witness or the victim of atrocity when called upon during hearing, investigation and trial of an offence under the Act.

(4) The witness, the victim of atrocity or his/her dependent and the attendant shall be paid daily maintenance expenses, for the days he/she is away from the place of his/her residence or stay during investigation, hearing and trial of an offence, at such rates but not less than the minimum wages, as may be fixed by the State Government for the agricultural labourers.

(5) In addition to daily maintenance expenses the witness, the victim of atrocity (or his/her dependent) and the attendant shall also be paid diet expenses at such rates as may be fixed by the State Government from time to time.

(6) The payment of travelling allowance, daily allowance, maintenance expenses and reimbursement of transport facilities shall be made immediately or not later than three days by the District Magistrate or the Sub-Divisional Magistrate or any other Executive Magistrate to the victim their dependents/attendants and witnesses for the days they visit the investigating officer or in-charge police station or hospital authorities or Superintendent of Police/Deputy Superintendent of Police, or District Magistrate or any other officer concerned or the Special Court.

(7) When an offence has been committed under Section 3 of the Act, the District Magistrate or the Sub-Divisional Magistrate or any other Executive Magistrate shall reimburse the payment of medicines, special medical consultation, blood transfusion, placement of essential clothing, meals and fruits provided to the victim(s) of atrocity.

12. Measures to be taken by the District Administration –

(1) The District Magistrate and the Superintendent of Police shall visit the place or area where the atrocity has been committed to assess the loss of life and damage to the property and draw a list of victims, their family members and dependents entitled for relief.

(2) Superintendent of Police shall ensure that the First Information Report is registered in the book of the concerned police station and effective measures for apprehending the accused are taken.

(3) The Superintendent of Police, after spot inspection, shall immediately appoint an investigation officer and deploy such police force in the area and take such other preventive measures as he may deem proper necessary.

(4) The District Magistrate or the Sub-Divisional Magistrate or any other Executive Magistrate shall make arrangements for providing immediate relief in cash or in kind or both to the victims of atrocity, their family members and dependents according to the scale as in the Schedule annexed to these rules (Annexure I read with Annexure II). Such immediate relief shall also include food, water, clothing, shelter, medical aid, transport facilities and other essential items necessary for human beings.

(5) The relief provided to the victim of the atrocity or his/her dependent under sub-rule (4) in respect of death, or injury to, or damage to property shall be in addition to any other right to claim compensation in respect thereof under any other law for the time being in force.

(6) The relief and rehabilitation facilities mentioned in sub-rule (4) above shall be provided by the District Magistrate or the Sub-Divisional Magistrate or any other Executive Magistrate in accordance with the scales provided in the Schedule annexed to these rules.

(7) A report of the relief and rehabilitation facilities provided to the victims shall also be forwarded to the Special Court by the District Magistrate or the Sub-Divisional Magistrate or any other Executive Magistrate or Superintendent of Police. In case the Special Court is satisfied that the payment of relief was not made to the victim or his/her dependent in time or the amount of relief or compensation was not sufficient or only a part of payment of relief or compensation was made, it may order for making in full or part the payment of relief or any other kind of assistance.

13. Selection of officers and other staff members for completing the work relating to atrocity –

(1) The State Government shall ensure that the administrative officers and other staff members to be appointed in an area prone to atrocity shall have the right aptitude and understanding of the problems of the Scheduled Castes and the Scheduled Tribes.

(2) It shall be ensured by the State Government that persons from the Scheduled Castes and the Scheduled Tribes are adequately represented in the administration and in the police force at all levels, particularly at the level of police posts and police station.

14. **Specific Responsibility of the State Government** – The State Government shall make necessary provisions in its annual budget for providing relief and rehabilitation facilities to the victims of atrocity. It shall review atleast twice in a calendar year, in the month of January and July the performance of the Special Public Prosecutor specified or appointed under Section 15 of the Act, various reports received, investigation made and preventive steps taken by the District Magistrate or the Sub-Divisional Magistrate and Superintendent of Police, relief and rehabilitation provided to the victims and the reports in respect of lapses on behalf of the concerned officers.

15. **Contingency Plan by the State Government** –

(1) The State Government shall prepare a model contingency plan for implementing the provisions of the Act and notify the same in the Official Gazette of the State Government. It should specify the role and responsibility of various departments and their officers at different levels, the role and responsibility of Rural/Urban Local Bodies and Non-Government Organisation. *Inter alia* this plan shall contain a package of relief measures including the following:

(a) scheme to provide immediate relief in cash or in kind or both;

(b) allotment of agricultural land and house sites;

(c) the rehabilitation packages;

(d) scheme for employment in Government or Government undertaking to the dependent or one of the family members of the victim;

(e) pension scheme for widows, dependent children of the deceased, handicapped or old age victims of atrocity;
(f) mandatory compensation for the victims;
(g) scheme for strengthening the socio-economic condition of the victim;
(h) provisions for providing brick/stone masonry house to the victims;
(i) such other elements as health care, supply of essential commodities, electrification, adequate drinking water facility, burial/cremation ground and link road to Scheduled Castes and the Scheduled Tribes habitats.

(2) The State Government shall forward a copy of the contingency plan or summary thereof and a copy of the scheme, as soon as may be, to the Central Government in the Ministry of Welfare and to all the District Magistrates, sub-Divisional Magistrates, Inspectors General of Police and Superintendents of Police.

16. Constitution of State-level vigilance and monitoring committee –

(1) The State Government shall constitute a high power vigilance and monitoring committee of not more than 25 members consisting of the following:

(i) Chief Minister/Administrator – Chairman (in case of a State under President's Rule Governor – Chairman);
(ii) Home Minister, Finance Minister and Welfare Minister – Members (in case of a State under the President's Rule Advisors – Members);
(iii) all elected members of Parliament and State Legislative Assembly and Legislative Council from the State belonging to the Scheduled Caste and the Scheduled Tribe – Members;

(iv) Chief Secretary, the Home Secretary, the Director General of Police, Director, Deputy Director National Commission for the Scheduled Castes and the Scheduled Tribes – Members;

(v) the Secretary in-charge of the welfare and development of the Scheduled Castes and the Scheduled Tribes – Convenor.

(2) The high power vigilance and monitoring committee shall meet at least twice in a calendar year, in the month of January and July to review the implementation of the provisions of the Act, relief and rehabilitation facilities provided to the victims and other matters connected therewith, prosecution of cases under the Act, role of different officers/ agencies responsible for implementing the provisions of the Act and various reports received by the State Government.

17. Consultation of district-level vigilance and monitoring committee –

(1) In each district within the State, the District Magistrate shall set up a vigilance and monitoring committee in his district to review the implementation of the provisions of the Act, relief and rehabilitation facilities provided to the victims and other matters connected therewith, prosecution of cases under the Act, role of different officers/ agencies responsible for implementing the provisions of the Act and various reports received by the District Administration.

(2) The district-level vigilance and monitoring committee shall consist of elected members of the Parliament and State Legislative Assembly and Legislative Council, Superintendent of Police, three group 'A' officers/Gazetted officers of the State Government belonging to the Scheduled Castes and the Scheduled Tribes, not more than 5 non-official members belonging to the Scheduled Castes and the Scheduled Tribes and not more than 3 members from the categories other

than the Scheduled Castes and the Scheduled Tribes having association with Non-Governmental Organisations. The District Magistrate and District Social Welfare Officer shall be Chairman and Member-Secretary respectively.

(3) The district-level committee shall meet at least once in three months.

18. Material for annual report – The State Government shall every year before 31st March, forward the report to the Central Government about the measures taken for implementing provisions of the Act and various schemes/ plans framed by it during the previous calendar year.

ANNEXURE – I

SCHEDULE

[*See* Rule 12(4)]

Norms for Relief Amount

S. No.	Name of Offence	Minimum amount of relief
1.	Drink or eat inedible or obnoxious Substance [Section 3(1)(i)]	Rs. 25,000 or more depending upon the nature and gravity of the offence to each victim and also commensurate with the indignity, insult and defamation suffered by the victim.
2.	Causing injury, insult or annoyance [Section 3(1)(ii)]	
3.	Derogatory act [Section 3(1)(iii)]	Payment to be made as follows: I. 25 per cent when the charge-sheet is sent to the court. II. 75 per cent when accused are convicted by the lower court

S. No.	Name of Offence	Minimum amount of relief
4.	Wrongful occupation or cultivation of land etc.[Section 3(1)(iv)]	Atleast Rs. 25,000 or more depending upon the nature and gravity of the offence.
5.	Relating to land premises and water [Section 3(1)(v)]	The land/premises/water supply shall be restored where necessary at Government cost. Full payment to be made when charge-sheet is sent to the court.
6.	Begar or forced or bonded labour [Section 3(1)(vi)]	Atleast Rs. 25,000 to each victim, payment of 25% at FIR stage and 75 per cent on conviction in the lower court.
7.	Relating to right to franchise [Section 3(1)(vii)]	Upto Rs.20,000 to each victim depending upon the nature and gravity of the offence.
8.	False, malicious or vexatious legal proceedings [Section 3(1)(viii)]	Rs. 25,000 or reimbursement of actual legal expenses and damages or whichever is less after conclusion of the trial of the accused.
9.	False and frivolous information [Section 3(1)(ix)]	
10.	Insult, Intimidation and humiliation [Section 3(1)(x)]	Upto Rs.25,000 to each victim depending upon the nature of the offence. Payment of 25% when charge-sheet is sent to the court and rest on conviction.

S. No.	Name of Offence	Minimum amount of relief
11.	Outraging the modesty of a woman [Section 3(1)(xi)]	Rs. 50,000 to each victim of the offence. 50 per cent of the amount may be paid after medical examination and remaining 50 per cent at the conclusion of the trial.
12.	Sexual exploitation of a woman [Section 3(1)(xii)]	
13.	Fouling of Water [Section 3(1)(xiii)]	Upto Rs 1,00,000 or full cost of restoration of normal facility, including cleaning when the water is fouled. Payment may be made at the stage as deemed fit by District Administration.
14.	Denial of customary rights of passage [Section 3(1)(xiv)]	Upto Rs 1,00,000 or full cost of restoration of right of passage and full compensation of the loss suffered, if any. Payment of 50 per cent when charge-sheet is sent to the court and 50 per cent on conviction in lower court.
15.	Making one desert place of residence [Section 3(1)(xv)]	Restoration of the site/right to stay and compensation of Rs. 25,000 to each victim and reconstruction of the house at Government cost, if destroyed, to be paid in full when charge-sheet is sent to the lower court.

S. No. Name of Offence	Minimum amount of relief
16. Giving false evidence [Section 3(2)(i) and (ii)]	At least Rs. 1,00,000 or full compensation of the loss or harm sustained. 50 per cent to be paid when charge-sheet is sent to the court and 50 per cent on conviction by the lower court.
17. Committing offences under the Indian Penal Code punishable with imprisonment for a term of 10 years or more [Section 3(2)]	At least Rs. 50,000 depending upon the nature and grvity of the offence to each victim and/or his dependents. The amount would vary if specifically otherwise provided in the Schedule.
18. Victimization at the hands of a public servant [Section 3(2) (vii)]	Full compensation on account of damages or loss or harm sustained. 50 per cent to be paid when charge-sheet is sent to the court and 50 per cent on conviction by lower court.
19. *Disability*: The definitions of physical and mental disabilities are contained in the Ministry of Welfare, G.O.I. notification No. 4-2/83-HW.III dated 6.8. 1986 as amended from time to time.	

S. No.	Name of Offence	Minimum amount of relief
	(a) 100 per cent incapacitation:	
	(i) Non-earning Member of a family	Atleast Rs. 1,00,000 to each victim of offence. 50 per cent on FIR and 25 per cent at charge-sheet and 25% on conviction by the lower court.
	(ii) Earning Member of a Family	Atleast 2,00,000 to each victim of offence. 50 % to be paid on FIR/Medical examination stage, 25per cent when charge-sheet sent to court and 25 per cent at conviction in lower court.
	(b) Where incapacitation is less than 100 per cent	The rates as laid down in a (i) and (ii) above shall be reduced in the same proportion, the stages of payments also being the same. However, not less than Rs. 15,000 to non-earning member and not less than Rs. 30,000 to earning member of a family.
20.	Murder/Death	
	(i) Non-earning Member of a family.	At least Rs. 1,00,000 to each case. Payment of 75 per cent after postmortem and 25 per cent on conviction by the lower court.
	(ii) Earning Member of a Family	At least Rs.2,00,000 to each case. Payment of 75 per cent

S. No.	Name of Offence	Minimum amount of relief
		after postmortem and 25 per cent on conviction by the lower court.
21.	Victim of murder, death, massacre, rape, mass rape and gang rape, permanent incapacitation and dacoity.	In addition to relief amount paid under above items, relief may be arranged within three months of date of atrocity as follows:- (i) Pension to each widow and/or other dependents of deceased SC and ST @ Rs. 1,000 per month, or employment to one member of the family of the deceased, or provision of agricultural land, a house, if necessary by outright purchase. (ii) Full cost of the education and maintenance of the children of the victims. Children may be admitted to Ashram Schools/residential schools. (iii) Provision of utensils, rice, wheat, dals, pulses,etc. for a period of three months.
22.	Complete destruction/burnt houses	Brick/stone masonry house to be constructed or provided at government cost where it has been burnt or destroyed.

APPENDIX – III

The National Commission for Women Act, 1990

[30th August 1990]

An Act to constitute a National Commission for Women and to provide for matters connected therewith or incidental thereto.

Be it enacted by Parliament in the Forty-first Year of the Republic of India as Follows:

CHAPTER I
PRELIMINARY

1. Short Title, Extent and Commencement

(1) This Act may be called the National Commission for Women Act, 1990.

(2) It extends to the whole of India except the State of Jammu and Kashmir.

(3) It shall come into force on such date as the Central Government may, by notification in the Official Gazette, appoint.

2. Definitions

In this Act, unless the context otherwise requires,–

(a) "Commission" means the National Commission for women constituted under Section 3;

(b) "Member" means a Member of the Commission and includes the Member-Secretary;

(c) "Prescribed" means prescribed by rules under this Act.

CHAPTER II
THE NATIONAL COMMISSION FOR WOMEN

3. Constitution of the National Commission for Women

(1) The Central Government shall constitute a body to be known as the National Commission for Women to exercise the powers conferred on, to perform the functions assigned to it under this act.

(2) The Commission shall consist of –

(a) a Chairperson, committed to the cause of women, to be maintained by the Central Government;

(b) five Members to be nominated by the Central Government from amongst persons of ability, integrity and standing who have had experience in law or legislation, trade unionism, management of an industry or organisation committed to increasing the employment potential of women, women's voluntary organisations (including women activist), administration, economic development, health, education or social welfare:

Provided that at least one Member each shall be from amongst person belonging to the Scheduled Castes and Scheduled Tribes respectively;

(c) a Member-Secretary to be nominated by the Central Government, who shall be –

(i) an expert in the field of management, organisational structure or sociological movement, or

(ii) an officer who is a member of civil service of the Union or of an all-India service or holds a civil post under the Union with appropriate experience.

4. Term of Office and conditions of Service of Chairperson and Members

(1) The Chairperson and every member shall hold office for such period, not exceeding three years, as may be specified by the Central Government in this behalf.

(2) The Chairperson or a Member (other than the Member-Secretary who is a Member of civil service of the Union or of an all-India Service or holds a civil post under the Union) may, by writing and addressed to the Central Government, resign from the office of Chairperson or, as the case may be, of the member at any time.

(3) The Central Government shall remove a person from the office of Chairperson or Member referred to in sub-section (2) if that person–

(a) becomes an undischarged insolvent;

(b) gets convicted and sentenced to imprisonment for an offence which, in the opinion of the Central Government, involves moral turpitudes;

(c) becomes of unsound mind and stands so declared by a competent court;

(d) refuses to act or becomes incapable of acting;

(e) is, without obtaining leave of absence from the Commission, absent from three consecutive meetings of the Commission; or

(f) in the opinion of the Central Government has so abused the position of Chairperson or Member as to render that person's continuance in office detrimental to the public interest:

Provided that no person shall be removed under this clause until that person has been given reasonable opportunity of being heard in the matter.

(4) A vacancy caused under sub-section (2) or otherwise shall be filled by fresh nomination.

(5) The salaries and allowances payable to, and the other terms and conditions of service of, the Chairperson and Members shall be such as may be prescribed.

5. Officers and Other Employees of the Commission

(1) The Central Government shall provide the Commission with such officers and employees as may be necessary for the efficient performance of the functions of the Commission under this Act.

(2) The salaries and allowances payable to, and the other terms and conditions of service of, the officers and other employees appointed for the purpose of the Commission shall be such as may be prescribed.

6. Salaries and Allowances to be Paid out of Grants

The salaries and allowances payable to the Chairperson and Members and the administrative expenses, including salaries, allowances and pensions payable to the officers and other employees referred to in section 5, shall be paid out of grants referred to in sub-section (1) of section 11.

7. Vacancies, etc. not to invalidate Proceedings of the Commission

No act or proceeding of the Commission shall be questioned or shall be invalidated merely on the ground of the existence of any vacancy or defect in the constitution of the Commission.

8. Committees of the Commission

(1) The Commission may appoint such committees as may be necessary for dealing with such special issues as may be taken up by the Commission from time to time.

(2) The Commission shall have the power to co-opt as members of any committee appointed under sub-section (1) such number of persons, who are not Members of the Commission, as it may think fit and the persons so co-opted shall have the

right to attend the meetings of the committee and take part in its proceedings but shall not have the right to vote.

(3) The persons so co-opted shall be entitled to receive such allowance for attending the meetings of the committee as may be prescribed.

9. Procedure to be Regulated by the Commission

(1) The Commission or a committee thereof shall meet as and when necessary and shall meet at such time and place as the Chairperson may think fit.

(2) The Commission shall regulate its own procedure and the procedure of the committees thereof.

(3) All orders and decisions of the Commissions shall be authenticated by the Member-Secretary or any other officer of the Commission duly authorised by the Member-Secretary in this behalf.

CHAPTER III
FUNCTIONS OF THE COMMISSION

10 Functions of the Commission

(1) The Commission shall perform all or any of the following functions, namely:

(a) investigate and examine all matters relating to the safeguards provided for women under the Constitution and other laws;

(b) present to the Central Government, annually and at such other times as the Commission may deem fit, reports upon the working of those safeguards;

(c) make in such reports recommendations for the effective implementation of those safeguards for improving the conditions of women by the Union or any State;

(d) review, from time to time, the existing provisions of the Constitution and other laws affecting women and recommend amendments thereto so as to suggest remedial legislative measures to meet any lacunae, inadequacies or shortcomings in such legislation;

(e) take up the cases of violation of the provisions or the Constitution and of other laws relating to women with the appropriate authorities;

(f) look into complaints and take *suo motu* notice of matters relating to–

   (i) deprivation of women's rights;

   (ii) non-implementation of laws enacted to provide protection to women and also to achieve the objective of equality and development;

   (iii) non-compliance of policy decisions, guidelines or instructions aimed at mitigating hardships and ensuring welfare and providing relief to women, and take up the issues arising out of such matters with appropriate authorities;

(g) call for special studies or investigations into specific problems or situations arising out of discrimination and atrocities against women and identify the constraints so as to recommend strategies for their removal;

(h) undertake promotional and educational research so as to suggest ways of ensuring due representation of women in all spheres and identify factors responsible for impeding their advancement, such as, lack of access to housing and basic services, inadequate support services and technologies for reducing drudgery and occupational health hazards and for increasing their productivity;

(i) participate and advise on the planning process of socio-economic development of women;

(j) evaluate the progress of the development of women under the Union and any State;
(k) inspect or cause to be inspected a jail, remand home, women's institution or other place of custody where women are kept as prisoners or otherwise, and take up with the concerned authorities for remedial action, if found necessary;
(l) fund litigation involving issues affecting a large body of women;
(m) make periodical reports to the Government on any matter pertaining to women and in particular various difficulties under which women toil; and
(n) any other matter which may be referred to it by the Central Government.

(2) The Central Government shall cause all the reports referred to in clause (b) of sub-section (1) to be laid before each House of Parliament along with a memorandum explaining the action taken or proposed to be taken on the recommendations relating to the Union and the reasons for the non-acceptance, if any, of any of such recommendations.

(3) Where any such report or any part thereof relates to any matter with which any State Government is concerned, the Commission shall forward a copy of such report or part to such State Government who shall cause it to be laid before the Legislature of the State along with a memorandum explaining the action taken or proposed to be taken on the recommendations relating to the State and the reasons for the non-acceptance, if any, of any of such recommendations.

(4) The Commission shall, while investigating any matter referred to in clause (a) or sub-clause (i) of clause (f) of sub-section (1), have all the powers of civil court trying a suit and in particular, in respect of the following matters, namely:

(a) summoning and enforcing the attendance of any person from any part of India and examining him on oath;
(b) requiring the discovery and production of any document;
(c) receiving evidence on affidavits;
(d) requisitioning any public record or copy thereof from any court or office;
(e) issuing commissions for the examination of witnesses and documents; and
(f) any other matters which may be prescribed.

CHAPTER IV
FINANCE, ACCOUNTS AND AUDIT

11. Annual Report

The Commission shall prepare, in such form and at such time for each financial year, as may be prescribed, its annual report, giving a full account of its activities during the previous financial year and forward a copy thereof to the Central Government.

12. Annual Report and Audit Report to be Laid Before Parliament

The Central Government shall cause the annual report together with a memorandum of action taken on the recommendations contained therein, in so far as they relate to the Central Government, and the reasons for the non-acceptance, if any, of any of such recommendations and the audit report to be laid as soon as may be after the reports are received, before each House of Parliament.

CHAPTER V
MISCELLANEOUS

13. Chairperson, Members and Staff of the Commission to be Public Servants

The Chairperson, Members, officers and other employees of the Commission shall be deemed to be public servants within the meaning of section 21 of the Indian Penal Code.

14. Central Government to Consult Commission

The Central Government shall consult the Commission on all major policy matters affecting women.

15. Power to make Rules

(1) The Central Government may, by notification in the Official Gazette, make rules for carrying out the provisions of this Act.

(2) In particular, and without prejudice to the generality of the foregoing powers, such rules may provide for all or any of the following matters, namely:

(a) salaries and allowances payable to, and other terms and conditions of service of, the Chairperson and Members under sub-section (5) of section 4 and of officers and other employees under sub-section (2) of section 5;

(b) allowances for attending the meetings of the committee by the co-opted persons under sub-section (3) of section 8;

(c) other matters under clause (f) of sub-section (4) of section 10;

(d) the form in which the annual statement of accounts shall be maintained under sub-section (1) of section 12;

(e) the form in, and the time at, which the annual report shall be prepared under Section 13;

(f) any other matter which is required to be, or may be, prescribed.

(3) Every rule made under this Act shall be laid, as soon as may be after it is made, before each house of Parliament, while it is in session, for a total period of thirty days which may be comprised in one session or in two or more successive sessions, and if, before the expiry of the session immediately following the session or the successive sessions aforesaid, both Houses agree in making

any modification in the rule or both Houses agree that the rule should not be made, the rule shall thereafter have effect only in such modified form or be of no effect, as the case may be; so, however that any such modification or annulment shall be without prejudice to the validity of anything previously done under that rule.

APPENDIX – IV

The National Commission for Minorities Act, 1992

[17th May 1992]

An Act to constitute a National Commission for Minorities and to provide for matters connected therewith or incidental thereto.

Be it enacted by Parliament in the Forty-third Year of the Republic of India as follows:

CHAPTER I
PRELIMINARY

1. Short Title, Extent and Commencement

(1) This Act may be called the National Commission for Minorities Act, 1992.

(2) It extends to the whole of India except the State of Jammu and Kashmir.

(3) It shall come into force on such date as the Central Government may, by notification in the Official Gazette, appoint.

2. Definitions

In this Act, unless the context otherwise requires,–

(a) "Commission" means the National Commission for Minorities constituted under section 3;

(b) "Member" means a Member of the Commission and includes the vice-Chairperson;[1]

(c) "minority" for the purposes of this act, means a community

1. Inserted by the National Commission for Minorities Act, 1995 w.e.f. 8-9-95.

notified as such by the Central Government;

(d) "prescribed" means prescribed by rules made under this Act.

CHAPTER II
THE NATIONAL COMMISSION FOR MINORITIES

3. Constitution of National Commission for Minorities

(1) The Central Government shall constitute a body to be known as the National Commission for Minorities to exercise the powers conferred on, and to perform the functions assigned to, it under this act.

(2) The Commission shall consist of a Chairperson, a Vice Chairperson and five Members to be nominated by the Central Government from amongst persons of eminence, ability and integrity;

Provided that five Members including the Chairperson shall be from amongst the minority communities.

4. Term of Office and Conditions of Service of Chairperson and Members

(1) The Chairperson and every Member shall hold office for a term of three years from the date he assumes office.

(2) The Chairperson or a Member may, by writing under his hand addressed to the Central Government, resign from the office of Chairperson or, as the case may be, of the Member at any time.

(3) The Central Government shall remove a person from the office of Chairperson or Member referred to in sub-section (2) if that person–

(a) becomes an undischarged insolvent;

(b) is convicted and sentenced to imprisonment for an offence which, in the opinion of the Central Government, involves moral turpitudes;

(c) becomes of unsound mind and stands so declared by a competent court;

(d) refuses to act or becomes incapable of acting;

(e) is, without obtaining leave of absence from the Commission, absent from three consecutive meetings of the Commission; or

(f) has, in the opinion of the Central Government, so abused the position of Chairperson or Member as to render that person's continuance in office detrimental to the interests of minorities or the public interest:

Provided that no person shall be removed under this clause until that person has been given reasonable opportunity of being heard in the matter.

(4) A vacancy caused under sub-section (2) or otherwise shall be filled by fresh nomination.

(5) The salaries and allowances payable to, and the other terms and conditions of service of, the Chairperson and Members shall be such as may be prescribed.

5. Officers and Other Employees of the Commission

(1) The Central Government shall provide the Commission with a Secretary and such other officers and employees as may be necessary for the efficient performance of the functions of the Commission under this Act.

(2) The salaries and allowances payable to, and the other terms and conditions of service of, the officers and other employees appointed for the purpose of the Commission shall be such as may be prescribed.

6. Salaries and Allowances to be Paid out of Grants

The salaries and allowances payable to the Chairperson and Members and the administrative expenses, including salaries, allowances and pensions payable to the officers and other employees referred to in section 5, shall be paid out of grants referred to in sub-section (1) of section 10.

7. Vacancies, etc. not to Invalidate Proceedings of the Commission

No act or proceeding of the Commission shall be questioned or shall be invalidate merely on the ground of the existence of any vacancy or defect in the constitution of the Commission.

8. Procedure to be Regulated by the Commission

(1) The Commission shall meet as and when necessary at such time and place as the Chairperson may think fit.

(2) The Commission shall regulate its own procedure.

(3) All orders and decisions of the Commission shall be authenticated by the Secretary or any other officer of the Commission duly authorised by the Secretary in this behalf.

CHAPTER III
FUNCTIONS OF THE COMMISSION

9. Functions of the Commission

(1) The Commission shall perform all or any of the following functions, namely–

(a) evaluate the progress of the development of minorities under the Union and States;

(b) monitor the working of the safeguards provided in the Constitution and in laws enacted by Parliament and the State legislatures;

(c) make recommendations for the effective implementation of safeguards for the protection of the interests of minorities by the Central Government or the State Governments;

(d) look into specific complaints regarding deprivation of rights and safeguards of the minorities and take up such matters with the appropriate authorities;

(e) cause studies to be undertaken into problems arising out of any discrimination against minorities and recommend measures for their removal;

(f) conduct studies, research and analysis on the issues relating to socio-economic and educational development of minorities;

(g) suggest appropriate measures in respect of any minority to be undertaken by the Central Government or the State Governments;

(h) make periodical or special reports to the Central Government on any matter pertaining to minorities and in particular difficulties confronted by them; and

(i) any other matter which may be referred to it by the Central Government.

(2) The Central Government shall cause the recommendations referred to in clause (c) of sub-section (1) to be laid before each House of Parliament along with a memorandum explaining the action taken or proposed to be taken on the recommendations relating to the Union and the reasons for the non-acceptance, if any, of any of such recommendations.

(3) Where any recommendation referred to in clause (c) of sub-section (1) or any part thereof with which any State Government is concerned, the Commission shall forward a copy of such recommendation or part to such State Government who shall cause it to be laid before the Legislature of the State along with a memorandum explaining the action taken or proposed to be taken on the recommendations relating to the State and the reasons for the non-acceptance, if any, of any of such recommendation or part.

(4) The Commission shall, while performing any of the functions mentioned in sub-clauses (a), (b) and (d) of sub-section (1), have all the powers of civil court trying a suit and in particular, in respect of the following matters, namely–

(a) summoning and enforcing the attendance of any person from any part of India and examining him on oath;

(b) requiring the discovery and production of any document;
(c) receiving evidence on affidavits;
(d) requisitioning any public record or copy thereof from any court or office;
(e) issuing commissions for the examination of witnesses and documents; and
(f) any other matters which may be prescribed.

CHAPTER IV
FINANCE, ACCOUNTS AND AUDIT

10. Grants by the Central Government

(1) The Central Government shall, after due appropriation made by Parliament by law in this behalf, pay to the Commission by way of grants such sums of money as the Central Government may think fit for being utilised for the purposes of this Act.

(2) The Commission may spend such sums as it thinks fit for performing the functions under this Act, and such sums shall be treated as expenditure payable out of the grants referred to in sub-section (1).

11. Accounts and Audit

(1) The Commission shall maintain proper accounts and other relevant records and prepare an annual statement of accounts in such form as may be prescribed by the Central Government in consultation with the Comptroller and Auditor-General of India.

(2) The accounts of the Commission shall be audited by the Comptroller and Auditor-General at such intervals as may be specified by him and any expenditure incurred in connection with such audit shall be payable by the Commission to the Comptroller and Auditor-General.

(3) The Comptroller and Auditor-General and any person appointed by him in connection with the audit of the accounts of the Commission under this Act shall have

the same rights and privileges and the authority in connection with such audit as the Comptroller and Auditor-General generally has in connection with the audit of Government accounts and, in particular, shall have the right to demand the production of books, accounts, connected vouchers and other documents and papers and to inspect any of the offices of the Commission.

12. Annual Report

The Commission shall prepare, in such form and at such time, for each financial year, as may be prescribed, its annual report, giving a full account of its activities during the previous financial year and forward a copy thereof to the Central Government.

13. Annual Report and Audit Report to be Laid before Parliament

The Central Government shall cause the annual report together with a memorandum of action taken on the recommendations contained therein, in so far as they relate to the Central Government, and the reasons for the non-acceptance, if any, of any of such recommendations and the audit to be laid as soon as may be after the reports are received, before each House of Parliament.

CHAPTER V
MISCELLANEOUS

14. Chairperson, Members and Staff of the Commission to be Public Servants

The Chairperson, Members and employees of the Commission shall be deemed to be public servants within the meaning of section 21 of the Indian Penal Code.

15. Power to make Rules

(1) The Central Government may, by notification in the Official Gazette, make rules for carrying out the provisions of this Act.

(2) In particular, and without prejudice to the generality of the foregoing powers, such rules may provide for all or any of the following matters, namely:

(a) salaries and allowances payable to, and other terms and conditions of service of, the Chairperson and Members under sub-section (5) of section 4 and of officers and other employees under sub-section (2) of section 5;

(b) any other matter under clause (f) of sub-section (4) of section 9;

(c) the form in which the annual statement of account shall be maintained under sub-section (1) of section 11;

(d) the form in, and the time at, which the annual report shall be prepared under section 12;

(e) any other matter which is required to be, or may be, prescribed.

(3) Every rule made under this Act shall be laid, as soon as may be after it is made, before each House of Parliament, while it is in session, for a total period of thirty days which may be comprised in one session or in two or more successive sessions, and if, before the expiry of the session immediately following the session or the successive sessions aforesaid, both Houses agree in making any modification in the rule or both Houses agree that the rule should not be made, the rule shall thereafter have effect only in such modified form or be of no effect, as the case may be; so, however, that any such modification of annulment shall be without prejudice to the validity of anything previously done under that rule.

16. Power to remove Difficulties

(1) If any difficulty arises in giving effect to the provisions of this Act, the Central Government may, by order published in the Official Gazette, make such provisions, not inconsistent with the provisions of this Act as appear to it to be necessary or expedient for removing the difficulty;

Provided that no such order shall be made after the expiry of period of two years from the date of commencement of this Act.

(2) Every order made under this section shall, as soon as may be after it is made, be laid before each House of Parliament.

APPENDIX - V

The National Commission for Backward Classes Act, 1993

(No. 27 of 1993)

[2nd April, 1993]

An Act to constitute a National Commission for Backward Classes other than the Scheduled Castes and the Scheduled Tribes and to provide for matters connected therewith or incidental thereto.

Be it enacted by Parliament in the Forty-fourth Year of the Republic of India as follows:

CHAPTER I
PRELIMINARY

1. Short Title, Extent and Commencement

(1) This Act may be called the National Commission for Backward Classes Act, 1993.

(2) It extends to the whole of India except the State of Jammu and Kashmir.

(3) It shall be deemed to have come into force on the 1st day of February, 1993.

2. Definitions

In this Act, unless the context otherwise requires,–

(a) "backward classes" means such backward classes of citizens other than the Scheduled Castes and the Scheduled Tribes as may be specified by the Central Government in the lists;

(b) "Commission" means the National Commission for Backward Classes constituted under Section 3;

(c) "lists" means lists prepared by the Government of India from time to time for purposes of making provision for the reservation of appointments or posts in favour of backward classes of citizens which, in the opinion of that Government, are not adequately represented in the services under the Government of India and any local or other authority within the territory of India or under the control of the Government of India;

(d) "Member" means a Member of the Commission and includes the Chairperson;

(e) "prescribed" means prescribed by rules under this Act.

CHAPTER II
THE NATIONAL COMMISSION FOR BACKWARD CLASSES

3. Constitution of the National Commission for Backward Classes

(1) The Central Government shall constitute a body to be known as the National Commission for Backward Classes to exercise the powers conferred on, and to perform the functions assigned to it, under this Act.

(2) The Commission shall consist of the following Members nominated by the Central Government:

(a) a Chairperson, who is or has been a Judge of the Supreme Court or of a High Court;

(b) a social scientist;

(c) two persons, who have special knowledge in matters relating to backward classes;

(d) a Member-Secretary, who is or has been an officer of the Central Government in the rank of a Secretary to the Government of India.

4. Term of Office and Conditions of Service of Chairperson and Members

(1) Every member shall hold office for a term of three years from the date he assumes office.

(2) A Member may, by writing under his hand addressed to the Central Government, resign from the office of Chairperson or, as the case may be, of Member at any time.

(3) The Central Government shall remove a person from the office of Member if that person –

(a) becomes an undischarged insolvent;

(b) gets convicted and sentenced to imprisonment for an offence which, in the opinion of the Central Government, involves moral turpitude;

(c) becomes of unsound mind and stands so declared by a competent court;

(d) refuses to act or becomes incapable of acting;

(e) is, without obtaining leave of absence from the Commission, absent from three consecutive meetings of the Commission;

(f) has, in the opinion of the Central Government, so abused the position of Chairperson or Member as to render that person's continuance in office detrimental to the interests of backward classes or the public interest:

Provided that no person shall be removed under this clause until that person has been given reasonable opportunity of being heard in the matter.

(4) A vacancy caused under sub-section (2) or otherwise shall be filled by fresh nomination.

(5) The salaries and allowances payable to, and the other terms and conditions of service of, the Chairperson and Members shall be such as may be prescribed.

5. Officers and Other Employees of the Commission

(1) The Central Government shall provide the Commission with such officers and employees as may be necessary for the

efficient performance of the functions of the Commission under this Act.

(2) The salaries and allowances payable to, and the other terms and conditions of service of, the officers and other employees appointed for the purpose of the Commission shall be such as may be prescribed.

6. Salaries and Allowances to be Paid out of Grants

The salaries and allowances payable to the Chairperson and Members and the administrative expenses, including salaries, allowances and pensions payable to the officers and other employees referred to in section 5, shall be paid out of grants referred to in sub-section (1) of section 12.

7. Vacancies, etc. not to Invalidate Proceedings of the Commission

No act or proceeding of the Commission shall be invalid merely on the ground of the existence of any vacancy or defect in the constitution of the Commission.

8. Procedure to be regulated by the Commission

(1) The Commission shall meet as and when necessary and shall meet at such time and place as the Chairperson may think fit.

(2) The Commission shall regulate its own procedure.

(3) All orders and decisions of the Commissions shall be authenticated by the Member-Secretary or any other officer of the Commission duly authorised by the Member-Secretary in this behalf.

CHAPTER III
FUNCTIONS AND POWERS OF THE COMMISSION

9. Functions of the Commission

(1) The Commission shall examine requests for inclusion of any class of citizens as a backward class in the lists and hear

complaints of over-inclusion or under-inclusion of any backward class in such lists and tender such advice to the Central Government as it deems appropriate.

(2) The advice of the Commission shall ordinarily be binding upon the Central Government.

10. Powers of the Commission

The Commission shall, while performing its functions under sub-section (1) of section 9, have all the powers of a civil court trying a suit and in particular, in respect of the following matters, namely:

(a) summoning and enforcing the attendance of any person from any part of India and examining him on oath;
(b) requiring the discovery and production of any document;
(c) receiving evidence on affidavits;
(d) requisitioning any public record or copy thereof from any court or office;
(e) issuing commissions for the examination of witnesses and documents; and
(f) any other matter which may be prescribed.

11. Periodic Revision of Lists by the Central Government

(1) The Central Government may at any time, and shall, at all expiration of ten years from the coming into force of this Act and every succeeding period of ten years thereafter, undertake revision of the lists with a view to excluding from such lists those classes who have ceased to be backward classes or for including in such lists new backward classes.

(2) The Central Government shall, while undertaking any revision referred to in sub-section (1), consult the Commission.

CHAPTER IV
FINANCE, ACCOUNTS AND AUDIT

12. Grants by the Central Government

(1) The Central Government shall, after due appropriation made by Parliament by law in this behalf, pay to the Commission by way of grants such sums of money as the Central Government may think fit for being utilised for the purposes of this Act.

(2) The Commission may spend such sums as it thinks fit for performing the functions under this Act, and such sums shall be treated as expenditure payable out of the grants referred to in sub-section (1).

13. Accounts and Audit

(1) The Commission shall maintain proper accounts and other relevant records and prepare an annual statement of accounts in such form as may be prescribed by the Central Government in consultation with the Comptroller and Auditor-General of India.

(2) The accounts of the Commission shall be audited by the Comptroller and Auditor-General at such intervals as may be specified by him and any expenditure incurred in connection with such audit shall be payable by the Commission to the Comptroller and Auditor-General.

(3) The Comptroller and Auditor-General and any person appointed by him in connection with the audit of the accounts of the Commission under this Act shall have the same rights and privileges and the authority in connection with such audit as the Comptroller and Auditor-General generally has in connection with the audit of Government accounts and, in particular, shall have the right to demand the production of books, accounts, connected vouchers and other documents and papers and to inspect any of the offices of the Commission.

14. Annual Report

The Commission shall prepare, in such form and at such time, for each financial year, as may be prescribed, its annual report, giving a full account of its activities during the previous financial year and forward a copy thereof to the Central Government.

15. Annual Report and Audit Report to be laid before Parliament

The Central Government shall cause the annual report together with a memorandum of action taken on the advice tendered by the Commission under Section 9, and the reasons for the non-acceptance, if any, of any such advice, and the audit report to be laid as soon as may be after the reports are received, before each House of Parliament.

CHAPTER V
MISCELLANEOUS

16. Chairperson, Members and Employees of the Commission to be Public Servants

The Chairperson, Members and employees of the Commission shall be deemed to be public servants within the meaning of section 21 of the Indian Penal Code.

17. Power to make Rules

(1) The Central Government may, by notification in the Official Gazette, make rules for carrying out the provisions of this Act.

(2) In particular, and without prejudice to the generality of the foregoing powers, such rules may provide for all or any of the following matters, namely:

(a) salaries and allowances payable to, and other terms and conditions of service of, the Chairperson and Members under sub-section (5) of section 4 and the officers and other employees under sub-section (2) of section 5;

(b) the form in which the annual statement of account shall be prepared under sub-section (1) of Section 13;

(c) the form in, and the time at, which the annual report shall be prepared under Section 14;

(d) any other matter which is required to be, or may be, prescribed.

(3) Every rule made under this Act shall be laid, as soon as may be after it is made, before each House of Parliament, while it is in session, for a total period of thirty days which may be comprised in one session or in two or more successive sessions, and if, before the expiry of the session immediately following the session or the successive sessions aforesaid, both Houses agree in making any modification in the rule or both Houses agree that the rule should not be made, the rule shall thereafter have effect only in such modified form or be of no effect, as the case may be; so, however, that any such modification or annulment shall be without prejudice to the validity of anything previously done under that rule.

18. Powers to remove difficulties

(1) If any difficulty arises in giving effect to the provisions of this Act, the Central Government may, by order published in the Official Gazette, make such provisions, not inconsistent with the provisions of this Act as appear to it to be necessary or expedient for removing the difficulty:

Provided that no such order shall be made after the expiry of period of two years from the date of commencement of this Act.

(2) Every order made under this section shall, as soon as may be after it is made, be laid before each House of Parliament.

19. Repeal and Saving

(1) The National Commission for Backward Classes Ordinance, 1993 is hereby repealed.

(2) Notwithstanding such repeal, anything done or any action taken under the said Ordinance, shall be deemed to have been done or taken under the corresponding provisions of this Act.

APPENDIX - VI

The Protection of Human Rights Act, 1993

[8th January, 1994]

An Act to provide for the Constitution of a National Human Rights Commission, State Human Rights Commissions in States and Human Rights Courts for better protection of human rights and for matters connected therewith or incidental thereto.

Be it enacted by Parliament in the Forty-fourth Year of the Republic of India as follows:

CHAPTER I
PRELIMINARY

1. Short Title, Extent and Commencement

(1) This Act may be called the Protection of Human Rights Act, 1993.

(2) It extends to the whole of India.

(3) It shall be deemed to have come into force on the 28th day of September, 1993.

2. Definitions

(1) In this Act, unless the context otherwise requires,–

(a) "armed forces" means the naval, military and air forces and includes any other armed forces of the Union;

(b) "Chairperson" means the Chairperson of the Commission or of the State Commission, as the case may be;

(c) "Commission" means the National Human Rights Commission constituted under Section 3;

(d) "human rights" means the rights relating to life, liberty, equality and dignity of the individual guaranteed by the Constitution or embodied in the International Covenants and enforceable by Courts in India;

(e) "Human Rights Courts" means the Human Rights Court specified under Section 30;

(f) "International Covenants" means the International Covenant on Civil and Political Rights and the International Covenants on Economic, Social and Cultural Rights adopted by the General Assembly of the United Nations on the 16th December, 1966;

(g) "Member" means a Member of the Commission or of the State Commission, as the case may be, and includes the Chairperson;

(h) "National Commission for Minorities" means the National Commission for Minorities constituted under Section 3 of the National Commission for Minorities Act, 1992;

(i) "National Commission for the Scheduled Castes and Scheduled Tribes" means the National Commission for the Scheduled Castes and Scheduled Tribes referred to in Article 338 of the Constitution;

(j) "National Commission for Women" means the National Commission for Women constituted under Section 3 of the National Commission for Women Act, 1990;

(k) "notification" means a notification published in the Official Gazette;

(l) "prescribed" means prescribed by rules made under the Act;

(m) "public servant" shall have the meaning assigned to it in section 21 of the Indian Penal Code;

(n) "State Commission" means a State Human Rights Commission constituted under section 21.

(2) Any reference in this Act to a law, which is not in force in the State of Jammu and Kashmir, shall, in relation to that State, be construed as a reference to a corresponding law, if any, in force in that State.

CHAPTER II
THE NATIONAL HUMAN RIGHTS COMMISSION

3. Constitution of a National Human Rights Commission

(1) The Central Government shall constitute a body to be known State of Jammu and Kashmir, shall in relation to that State, be conferred upon, and to perform the functions assigned to it, under this Act.

(2) The Commission shall consist of–

(a) a Chairperson who has been a Chief Justice of the Supreme Court;

(b) one Member who, is or has been, a judge of the Supreme Court;

(c) one member who is, or has been, the Chief Justice of a High Court;

(d) two Members to be appointed from amongst persons having knowledge of, or practical experience in, matters relating to human rights;

(3) The Chairperson of the National Commission for Minorities, the National Commission for the Scheduled Castes and Scheduled Tribes and the National Commission for Women shall be deemed to be Members of the Commission for the discharge of functions specified in clauses (b) to (j) of section 12.

(4) There shall be a Secretary-General who shall be the Chief Executive Officer of the Commission and shall exercise such powers and discharge such functions of the Commission as it may delegate to him.

(5) The headquarters of the Commission shall be at Delhi and the Commission may, with the previous approval of the Central Government, establish offices at other places in India.

4. Appointment of Chairperson and Other Members

(1) The Chairperson and other Members shall be appointed by the President by warrant under his hand and seal:

Provided that every appointment under this sub-section shall be made after obtaining the recommendations of a Committee consisting of–

(a)	the Prime Minister	-	Chairperson;
(b)	Speaker of the House of the People	-	Member;
(c)	Minister-in-charge of the Ministry of Home Affairs in the Government of India	-	Member;
(d)	Leader of the Opposition in the House of the People	-	Member;
(e)	Leader of the Opposition in the Council of States	-	Member;
(f)	Deputy Chairman of the Council of States	-	Member;

Provided further that no sitting Judge of the Supreme Court or sitting Chief Justice of a High Court shall be appointed except after consultation with the Chief Justice of India.

(2) No appointment of a Chairperson or a Member shall be invalid merely by reason of any vacancy in the Committee.

5. Removal of a Member of the Commission

(1) Subject to the provisions of sub-sections (2), the Chairperson or any other Member of the Commission shall only be removed from his office by order of the President on the ground of proved misbehaviour or incapacity after the Supreme Court, on reference being made to it by the President, has, on inquiry held in accordance with the procedure prescribed in that behalf by the Supreme Court, reported that the Chairperson or such other Member, as the case may be, ought on any such ground to be removed.

(2) Notwithstanding anything in sub-section (1), the President may by order remove from office the Chairperson or any other member if the Chairperson or such other Member, as the case may be,–

(a) is adjudged an insolvent; or

(b) engages during his term of office in any paid employment outside the duties of his office; or

(c) is unfit to continue in office by reason of infirmity of mind or body; or

(d) is of unsound mind and stands so declared by a competent court; or

(e) is convicted and sentenced to imprisonment for an offence which in the opinion of the President involves moral turpitude.

6. Term of Office of Members

(1) A person appointed as Chairperson shall hold office for a term of five years from the date on which he enters upon his office or until he attains the age of seventy years, whichever is carlier.

(2) A person appointed as Member shall hold office for a term of five years from the date on which he enters upon his office and shall be eligible for re-appointment for another term of five years.

Provided that no Member shall hold office after he has attained the age of seventy years.

(3) On ceasing to hold office, a Chairperson or a Member shall be ineligible for further employment under the government of India or under the Government of any State.

7. Member to Act as Chairperson or to Discharge his Functions in Certain Circumstances

(1) In the event of the occurrence of any vacancy in the office of the Chairperson by reason of his death, resignation or otherwise, the President may, by notification, authorise one of the Members to act as the Chairperson until the appointment of a new Chairperson to fill such vacancy.

(2) When the Chairperson is unable to discharge his functions owing to absence on leave or otherwise, such one of the Members as the President may, by notification, authorise in this behalf, shall discharge the functions of the Chairperson until the date on which the Chairperson resumes his duties.

8. Terms and Conditions of Service of Members

The salaries and allowances payable to, and other terms and conditions of service of, the member shall be such as may be prescribed:

Provided that neither the salary and allowances nor the other terms and conditions of service of a Member shall be varied to his disadvantage after his appointment.

9. Vacancies, etc. not to Invalidate the Proceedings of the Commission

No act of proceedings of the Commission shall be questioned or shall be invalidated merely on the ground of existence of any vacancy or defect in the constitution of the Commission.

10. Procedure to be regulated by the Commission

(1) The Commission shall meet at such time and place as the Chairperson may think fit.

(2) The Commission shall regulate its own procedure.

(3) All orders and decisions of the Commission shall be authenticated by the Secretary-General or any other officer of the Commission duly authorised by the Chairperson in this behalf.

11. Officers and Other Staff of the Commission

(1) The Central Government shall make available to the Commission–

(a) an officer of the rank of the Secretary to the Government of India who shall be the Secretary-General of the Commission; and

(b) such police and investigative staff under an officer not below the rank of a Director General of Police and such other officers and staff as may be necessary for the efficient performance of the functions of the Commission.

(2) Subject to such rules as may be made by the Central Government in this behalf, the Commission may appoint such other administrative, technical and scientific staff as it may consider necessary.

(3) The salaries, allowances and conditions of service of the officer and other staff appointed under sub-section (2) shall be such as may be prescribed.

CHAPTER III
FUNCTIONS AND POWERS OF THE COMMISSION

12. Functions of the Commission

The Commission shall perform all or any of the following functions, namely:

(a) inquire, *suo motu* or on a petition presented to it by a victim or any person on his behalf, into complaint of–

   (i) violation of human rights or abetment thereof; or
   (ii) negligence in prevention of such violation by a public servant;

(b) intervene in any proceeding involving any allegation of violation of human rights pending before a court with the approval of such court;
(c) visit, under intimation to the State Government, any jail or any other institution under the control of the State Government where persons are detained or lodged for purposes of treatment, reformation or protection to study the living conditions of the inmates and make recommendations thereon;
(d) review the safeguards provided by or under the Constitution or any law for the time being in force for the protection of human rights and recommend measures for their effective implementation;
(e) review the factors, including acts of terrorism, that inhibit the enjoyment of human rights and recommend appropriate remedial measures;
(f) study treaties and other international instruments on human rights and make recommendations for their effective implementation;
(g) undertake and promote research in the field of human rights;
(h) spread human rights literacy among various sections of society and promote awareness of the safeguards available for the protection of these rights through publications, the media, seminars and other available means;
(i) encourage the efforts of non-governmental organisations and institutions working in the field of human rights;
(j) such other functions as it may consider necessary for the promotion of human rights.

13. Powers relating to Inquiries

(1) The Commission shall, while inquiring into complaints under this Act have all the powers of a civil court trying a suit under the code of Civil Procedure, 1908, and in particular in respect of the following matters, namely:

(a) summoning and enforcing the attendance of witnesses and examining them on oath;
(b) discovery and production of any document;
(c) receiving evidence on affidavits;
(d) requisitioning any public record or copy thereof from any court or office;
(e) issuing commissions for the examination of witnesses or documents;
(f) any other matter which may be prescribed.

(2) The Commission shall have power to require any person, subject to any privilege which may be claimed by that person under any law for the time being in force, to furnish information on such points or matters as, in the opinion of the Commission, may be useful for, or relevant to, the subject matter of the inquiry and any person so required shall be deemed to be legally bound to furnish such information within the meaning of section 176 and section 177 of the Indian Penal Code.

(3) The Commission or any other officer, not below the rank of a Gazetted Officer, specially authorised in this behalf by the Commission may enter any building or place where the Commission has reason to believe that any document relating to the subject matter of the inquiry may be found, and may seize any such document or take extracts or copies therefrom subject to the provisions of section 100 of the Code of Criminal Procedure, 1973, in so far as it may be applicable.

(4) The Commission shall be deemed to be a civil court and when any offence as is described in Section 175, Section 178, Section 179, Section 180 or Section 228 of the Indian

Penal Code is commuted in the view or presence of the Commission, the Commission may, after recording the facts constituting the offence and the statement of the accused as provided for in the Code of Criminal Procedure, 1973, forward the case to a Magistrate having jurisdiction to try the same and the Magistrate to whom any such case is forwarded shall proceed to hear the complaint against the accused as if the case has been forwarded to him under section 346 of the Code of Criminal Procedure, 1973.

(5) Every proceeding before the Commission shall be deemed to be a judicial proceeding within the meaning of Sections 193 and 228 and for the purposes of Section 196, of the Indian Penal Code, and the Commission shall be deemed to be a civil court for all the purposes of Section 195 and Chapter XXVI of the Code of Criminal Procedure, 1973.

14. Investigation

(1) The Commission may, for the purpose of conducting any investigation pertaining to the inquiry, utilise the services of any officer or investigation agency of the Central Government or any State Government with the concurrence of the Central Government or the State Government, as the case may be.

(2) For the purpose of investigating into any matter pertaining to the inquiry, any officer or agency whose services are utilised under sub-section (1) may, subject to the direction and control of the Commission,–

(a) summon and enforce the attendance of any person and examine him;

(b) require the discovery and production of any document; and

(c) requisition any public record or copy thereof from any office.

(3) The provisions of section 15 shall apply in relation to any statement made by a person before any officer or agency

whose services are utilised under sub-section (1) as they apply in relation to any statement made by a person in the course of giving evidence before the Commission.

(4) The officer or agency whose services are utilised under sub-section (1) shall investigate into any matter pertaining to the inquiry and submit a report thereon to the Commission within such period as may be prescribed by the Commission in this behalf.

(5) The Commission shall satisfy itself about the correctness of the facts stated and the conclusion, if any, arrived at in the report submitted to it under sub-section (4) and for this purpose the Commission may make such inquiry (including examination of the person or persons who conducted or assisted in the investigation) as it thinks fit.

15. Statement made by Persons to the Commission

No statement made by a person in the course of giving evidence before the Commission shall subject him to, or be used against him, in any civil or criminal proceedings except a prosecution for giving false evidence by such statement:

Provided that the statement–

(a) is made in reply to the question which he is required by the Commission to answer; or

(b) is relevant to the subject matter of the inquiry.

16. Persons likely to be prejudicially affected to be heard

If at any stage of the inquiry, the Commission–

(a) considers it necessary to inquire into the conduct of any person;

(b) is of the opinion that the reputation of any person is likely to be prejudicially affected by the inquiry,

it shall give to that person a reasonable opportunity of being heard in the inquiry and to produce evidence in his defence.

Provided that nothing in this section shall apply where the credit of a witness is being impeached.

CHAPTER IV
PROCEDURE

17. Inquiry into Complaints

The Commission while inquiring into the complaints of violations of human rights may–

(i) call for information or report from the Central Government or any State Government or any other authority or organisation subordinate thereto within such time as may be specified by it:

Provided that –

(a) if the information or report is not received within the time stipulated by the Commission, it may proceed to inquire into the complaint on its own;

(b) if, on the receipt of information or report, the Commission is satisfied either that no further inquiry is required or that the required action has been initiated or taken by the concerned Government or authority, it may not proceed with the complaint and inform the complainant accordingly.

(ii) without prejudice to anything contained in clause (i), if it considers necessary, having regard to the nature of the complaint, initiate an inquiry.

18. Steps after Inquiry

The Commission may take any of the following steps upon the completion of an inquiry held under this Act, namely:

(1) where the inquiry discloses, the Commission of violation of human rights, it may recommend to the concerned

government or authority the initiation of proceedings for prosecution or such other action as the Commission may deem fit against the concerned person or persons;

(2) approach the Supreme Court or the High Court concerned for such directions, orders or writs as that Court may deem necessary;

(3) recommend to the concerned Government or authority for the grant of such immediate interim relief to the victim or the members of his family as the Commission may consider necessary;

(4) Subject to the provisions of clause (5) provide a copy of the inquiry report to the petitioner or his representative;

(5) the Commission shall send a copy of its inquiry report together with its recommendations to the concerned Government or authority and the concerned Government or authority shall, within a period of one month, or such further time as the Commission may allow, forward its comments or the report, including the action taken or proposed to be taken thereon, to the Commission;

(6) the Commission shall publish its inquiry report together with the comments of the concerned Government or authority, if any, and the action taken or proposed to be taken by the concerned Government or authority on the recommendations of the Commission.

19. Procedure with respect to Armed Forces

(1) Notwithstanding anything contained in this Act, while dealing with complaints of violation of human rights by the members of the armed forces, the Commission shall adopt the following procedure, namely:

(a) it may, either on its own motion or on receipt of a petition, seek a report from the Central Government;

(b) after the receipt of the report, it may either not proceed with the complaint or, as the case may be, make its recommendations to that Government.

(2) The Central Government shall inform the Commission of the action taken on the recommendations within three months or such further time as the Commission may allow.

(3) The Commission shall publish its report together with its recommendations made to the Central Government and the action taken by the Government on such recommendations.

(4) The Commission shall provide a copy of the report published under sub-section (3) to the petitioner or his representatives.

20. Annual and Special Reports of the Commission

(1) The Commission shall submit an annual report to the Central Government and to the State Government concerned and may at any time submit special reports on any matter which in its opinion, is of such urgency or importance that it should not be deferred till submission of the annual report.

(2) The Central Government and the State Government, as the case may be, shall cause the annual and special reports of the Commission to be laid before each House of Parliament or the State Legislature respectively, as the case may be, along with a memorandum of action taken or proposed to be taken on the recommendations of the Commission and the reasons for non-acceptance of the recommendations, if any.

CHAPTER V
STATE HUMAN RIGHTS COMMISSION

21. Constitution of State Human Rights Commission

(1) A State Government may constitute a body to be known as the .... (name of the State) Human Rights Commission to exercise the powers conferred upon, and to perform the functions assigned to, a State Commission under this Chapter.

(2) The State Commission shall consist of–

(a) a Chairperson who has been a Chief Justice of a High Court;

(b) one member who is, or has been, a judge of the High Court;
(c) one member who is, or has been, a district judge in that State;
(d) two Members to be appointed from amongst persons having knowledge of, or practical experience in, matters relating to human rights.

(3) There shall be a Secretary who shall be the Chief Executive Officer of the State Commission and shall exercise such powers and discharge such functions of the State Commission as it may delegate to him.
(4) The headquarters of the State Commission shall at such place as the State Government may, by notification, specify.
(5) A State Commission may inquire into violation of human rights only in respect of matters relatable to any of the entries enumerated in List II and List III in the Seventh Schedule to the Constitution.

Provided that if any such matter is already being inquired into by the Commission or any other Commission duly constituted under any law for the time being in force, the State Commission shall not inquire into the said matter:

Provided further that in relation to the Jammu and Kashmir Human Rights Commission, this sub-section shall have effect as if for the words and figures "List II and List III", the words and figures "List III, as applicable to the State of Jammu and Kashmir" had been substituted.

22. Appointment of Chairperson and Other Members of State Commission

(1) The Chairperson and other Members shall be appointed by the Governor by warrant under his hand and seal:

Provided that every appointment under this sub-section shall be made after obtaining the recommendations of a Committee consisting of–

(a)	the Chief Minister	–	Chairperson;
(b)	Speaker of the Legislative Assembly	–	Member;
(c)	Minister-in-charge of the Department of Home in that State	–	Member;
(d)	Leader of the Opposition in the Legislative Assembly	–	Member;

Provided further that where there is a Legislative Council in a State, the Chairman of that Council and the Leader of the Opposition in that Council shall also be members of the Committee:

Provided also that no sitting Judge of a High Court or a sitting district judge shall be appointed except after consultation with the Chief Justice of the High Court of the concerned State.

(2) No appointment of a Chairperson or a Member of the State Commission shall be invalid merely by reason of any vacancy in the Committee.

23. Removal of a Member of the State Commission

(1) Subject to the provisions of sub-sections (2), the Chairperson or any other Member of the State Commission shall only be removed from his office by order of the President on the ground of proved misbehaviour or incapacity after the Supreme Court, on a reference being made to it by the President, has, on inquiry held in accordance with the procedure prescribed in that behalf by the Supreme Court, reported that the Chairperson or such other Member, as the case may be, ought on any such ground to be removed.

(2) Notwithstanding anything in sub-section (1), the President may by order remove from office the Chairperson or any other member if the Chairperson or such other Member, as the case may be,–

(a) is adjudged an insolvent; or
(b) engages during his term of office in any paid employment outside the duties of his office; or
(c) is unfit to continue in office by reason of infirmity of mind or body; or
(d) is of unsound mind and stands so declared by a competent court; or
(e) is convicted and sentenced to imprisonment for an offence which in the opinion of the President involves moral turpitude.

24. Term of Office of Members of the State Commission

(1) A person appointed as Chairperson shall hold office for a term of five years from the date on which he enters upon his office or until he attains the age of seventy years, whichever is earlier.

(2) A person appointed as Member shall hold office for a term of five years from the date on which he enters upon his office and shall be eligible for re-appointment for another term of five years;

Provided that no Member shall hold office after he has attained the age of seventy years.

(3) On ceasing to hold office, a Chairperson or a member shall be ineligible for further employment under the Government of a State or under the Government of India.

25. Member to Act as Chairperson or to discharge his Functions in Certain Circumstances

(1) In the event of the occurrence of any vacancy in the office of the Chairperson by reason of his death, resignation or otherwise, the Governor may, by notification, authorise one of the Members to act as the Chairperson until the appointment of a new Chairperson to fill such vacancy.

(2) When the Chairperson is unable to discharge his functions owing to absence on leave or otherwise, such one of the Members as the Governor may, by notification, authorise in this behalf, shall discharge the functions of the Chairperson until the date on which the Chairperson resumes his duties.

26. Terms and Conditions of Service of Members of the State Commission

The salaries and allowances payable to, and other terms and conditions of service of, the Member shall be such as may be prescribed by the State Government:

Provided that neither the salary and allowances nor the other terms and conditions of service of a Member shall be varied to his disadvantage after his appointment.

27. Officers and Other Staff of the State Commission

(1) The State Government shall make available to the Commission–

(a) an officer not below the rank of the Secretary to the State Government who shall be the Secretary of the State Commission; and

(b) such police and investigative staff under an officer not below the rank of an Inspector General of Police and such other Officers and staff as may be necessary for the efficient performance of the functions of the Commission.

(2) Subject to such rules as may be made by the State Government in this behalf, the State Commission may appoint such other administrative, technical and scientific staff as it may consider necessary.

(3) The salaries, allowances and conditions of service of the officers and other staff appointed under sub-section (2) shall be such as may be prescribed by the State Government.

28. Annual and Special Reports of State Commission

(1) The State Commission shall submit an annual report to the State Government and may at any time submit special reports on any matter which, in its opinion, is of such urgency or importance that it should not be deferred till submission of the annual report.

(2) The State Government shall cause the annual and special reports of the State Commission to be laid before each House of State Legislature where it consists of Two Houses or where such Legislature consists of one House, before that House along with a memorandum of action taken or proposed to be taken on the recommendations of the State Commission and the reasons for non-acceptance of the recommendations, if any.

29. Application of Certain Provisions relating to National Human Rights Commission to State Commissions

The provision of Sections 9, 10, 12, 13, 14, 15, 16, 17 and 18 shall apply to a State Commission and shall have effect, subject to the following modifications, namely:

(a) references to "Commission" shall be construed as references to "State Commission";

(b) in section 10, in sub-section (3), for the word "Secretary-General", the word "Secretary" shall be substituted;

(c) in section 12, clause (f) shall be omitted;

(d) in section 17, in clause (i), the words "Central Government or any" shall be omitted.

CHAPTER VI
HUMAN RIGHTS COURTS

30. Human Rights Courts

For the purpose of speedy trial of offences arising out of violation of human rights, the State Government may, with the concurrence of the Chief Justice of the High Court, by notification, specify for each district a Court of Sessions to be a Human Rights Court to try the said offences:

Provided that nothing in this section shall apply if–

(a) a Court of Sessions is already specified as a special court; or

(b) a special court is already constituted,

for such offences under any other law for the time being in force.

31. Special Public Prosecutor

For every Human Rights Court, the State Government shall, by notification, specify a Public Prosecutor or appoint an advocate who has been in practice as an advocate for not less than seven years, as a Special Public Prosecutor for the purpose of conducting cases in that Court.

CHAPTER VII
FINANCE, ACCOUNTS AND AUDIT

32. Grants by the Central Government

(1) The Central Government shall, after due appropriation made by Parliament by law in this behalf, pay to the Commission by way of grants such sums of money as the Central Government may think fit for being utilised for the purposes of this Act.

(2) The Commission may spend such sums as it thinks fit for performing the functions under this Act, and such sums shall be treated as expenditure payable out of the grants referred to in sub-section (1).

33. Grants by the State Government

(1) The State Government shall, after due appropriation made by Legislature by law in this behalf, pay to the Commission by way of grants such sums of money as the State

Government may think fit for being utilised for the purposes of this Act.

(2) The State Commission may spend such sums as it thinks fit for performing the functions under Chapter V, and such sums shall be treated as expenditure payable out of the grants referred to in sub-section (1).

34. Accounts and Audit

(1) The Commission shall maintain proper accounts and other relevant records and prepare an annual statement of accounts in such form as may be prescribed by the Central Government in consultation with the Comptroller and Auditor-General of India.

(2) The accounts of the Commission shall be audited by the Comptroller and Auditor-General at such intervals as may be specified by him and any expenditure incurred in connection with such audit shall be payable by the Commission to the Comptroller and Auditor-General.

(3) The Comptroller and Auditor-General and any person appointed by him in connection with the audit of the accounts of the Commission under this Act shall have the same rights and privileges and the authority in connection with such audit as the Comptroller and Auditor-General generally has in connection with the audit of Government accounts and, in particular, shall have the right to demand the production of books, accounts, connected vouchers and other documents and papers and to inspect any of the offices of the Commission.

(4) The accounts of the Commission, as certified by the Comptroller and Auditor-General or any other person appointed by him in this behalf, together with the audit report thereon shall be forwarded annually to the Central Government by the Commission and the Central Government shall cause the audit report to be laid, as soon as may be, after it is received, before each House of Parliament.

35. Accounts and Audit of State Commission

(1) The State Commission shall maintain proper accounts and other relevant records and prepare an annual statement of accounts in such form as may be prescribed by the State Government in consultation with the Comptroller and Auditor-General of India.

(2) The accounts of the State Commission shall be audited by the Comptroller and Auditor-General at such intervals as may be specified by him and any expenditure incurred in connection with such audit shall be payable by the State Commission to the Comptroller and Auditor-General.

(3) The Comptroller and Auditor-General and any person appointed by him in connection with the audit of the accounts of the Commission under this Act shall have the same rights and privileges and the authority in connection with such audit as the Comptroller and Auditor-General generally has in connection with the audit of Government accounts and, in particular, shall have the right to demand the production of books, accounts, connected vouchers and other documents and papers and to inspect any of the offices of the State Commission.

(4) The accounts of the State Commission, as certified by the Comptroller and Auditor-General or any other person appointed by him in this behalf, together with the audit report thereon shall be forwarded annually to the State Government by the State Commission and the State Government shall cause the audit report to be laid, as soon as may be, after it is received, before the Legislature.

CHAPTER VIII
MISCELLANEOUS

36. Matters not Subject to Jurisdiction of the Commission

(1) The Commission shall not inquire into any matter which is pending before a State Commission or any other Commission duly constituted under any law for the time being in force.

(2) The Commission or the State Commission shall not inquire into any matter after the expiry of one year from the date on which the act constituting violation of human rights is alleged to have been committed.

37. Constitution of Special Investigation Teams

Notwithstanding anything contained in any other law for the time being in force, where the Government considers it necessary so to do, it may constitute one or more special investigation teams, consisting of such police officers as it thinks necessary for purposes of investigation and prosecution of offences arising out of violation of human rights.

38. Protection of Action taken in Good Faith

No suit or other legal proceeding shall lie against the Central Government, State Government, Commission, State Commission or any Member thereof or any person acting under the direction either of the Central Government, State Government, Commission or the State Commission in respect of anything which is in good faith done or intended to be done in pursuance of this Act or of any rules or any order made thereunder or in respect of the publication by or under the authority of the Central Government, State Government, Commission or the State Commission of any report, paper of proceedings.

39. Members and Officers to be Public Servants

Every Member of the Commission, State Commission and every officer appointed or authorised by the Commission or the State Commission to exercise functions under this Act shall be deemed to be a public servant within the meaning of section 21 of the Indian Penal Code.

40. Power of Central Government to make Rules

(1) The Central Government may, by notification in the Official Gazette, make rules for carrying out the provisions of this Act.

(2) In particular, and without prejudice to the generality of the foregoing powers, such rules may provide for all or any of the following matters, namely:

(a) the salaries and allowances payable to, and other terms and conditions of service of the Members under Section 8;

(b) the conditions subject to which other administrative, technical and scientific staff may be appointed by the Commission and the salaries and allowances of officers and other staff under sub-section (3) of section 11;

(c) any other power of a civil court required to be prescribed under clause (f) of sub-section (1) of section 13;

(d) the form in which the annual statement of accounts is to be prepared by the Commission under sub-section (1) of section 34; and

(e) any other matter which has to be, or may be, prescribed.

(3) Every rule made under this Act shall be laid, as soon as may be after it is made, before each house of Parliament, while it is in session, for a total period of thirty days which may be comprised in one session or in two or more successive sessions, and if, before the expiry of the session immediately following the session or the successive sessions aforesaid, both Houses agree in making any modification in the rule or both Houses agree that the rule should not be made, the rule shall thereafter have effect only in such modified form or be of no effect, as the case may be; so, however, that any such modification or annulment shall be without prejudice to the validity of anything previously done under that rule.

41. Power of State Government to make Rules

(1) The State Government may, by notification, make rules for carrying out the provisions of this Act.

(2) In particular, and without prejudice to the generality of the foregoing powers, such rules may provide for all or any of the following matters, namely:

(a) the salaries and allowances payable to, and other terms and conditions of service of the Members under section 26;

(b) the conditions subject to which other administrative, technical and scientific staff may be appointed by the Commission and the salaries and allowances of officers and other staff under sub-section (3) of section 27;

(c) the form in which the annual statement of accounts is to be prepared by the Commission under sub-section (1) of section 35.

(3) Every rule made by the State Government under this section shall be laid, as soon as may be after it is made, before each House of the State Legislature where it consists of two Houses, or where such Legislature consists of one House, before that House.

42. Power to remove difficulties

(1) If any difficulty arises in giving effect to the provisions of this Act, the Central Government may, by order published in the Official Gazette, make such provisions, not inconsistent with the provisions of this Act as appear to it to be necessary or expedient for removing the difficulty:

Provided that no such order shall be made after the expiry of the period of two years from the commencement of this Act.

(2) Every order made under this section shall, as soon as may be after it is made, be laid before each House of Parliament.

43. Repeal and Savings

(1) The Protection of Human Rights Ordinance, 1993 is hereby repealed.

(2) Notwithstanding such repeal anything done or any action taken under the said Ordinance shall be deemed to have been done or taken under the corresponding provisions of this Act.

APPENDIX - VII

The National Commission for Safai Karamcharis Act, 1993

[4th September, 1993]

An Act to constitute a National Commission for Safai Karamcharis and to provide for matters connected therewith or incidental thereto.

Be it enacted by Parliament in the Forty-fourth Year of the Republic of India as follows:

CHAPTER I
PRELIMINARY

1. Short Title, Extent, Application, Commencement, Duration and Savings

(1) This Act may be called the National Commission for Safai Karamcharis Act, 1993.

(2) It extends to the whole of India except the State of Jammu and Kashmir.

(3) It shall come into force on such date as the Central Government may, by notification in the Official Gazette, appoint.

(4) It shall cease to have effect after the 31st day of March, 1997[1] except as respects things done or omitted to be done before such cesser, and upon such section 6 of the General Clauses Act, 1897, shall apply as if this Act had than been repealed by a Central Act.

---

1. Extended for another five years.

2. Definitions

In this Act, unless the context otherwise requires,–

(a) "Chairperson" means the Chairperson of the Commission;

(b) "Commission" means the National Commission for Safai Karamcharis constituted under Section 3;

(c) "Member" means a Member of the Commission;

(d) "Prescribed" means prescribed by rules made under this Act;

(e) "Safai Karamchari" means a person engaged in, or employed for, manually carrying human excreta or any sanitation work;

(f) "Vice-Chairperson" means the Vice-Chairperson of the Commission.

CHAPTER II
THE NATIONAL COMMISSION FOR SAFAI KARAMCHARIS

3. Constitution of National Commission for Safai Karamcharis

(1) The Central Government shall, by notification in the Official Gazette, constitute a body to be known as the National Commission for Safai Karamcharis to exercise the powers conferred on, and to perform the functions assigned to, it under this Act.

(2) The Commission shall consist of–

(a) a Chairperson;

(b) a Vice-Chairperson;

(c) five members;

to be nominated, from amongst the persons of eminence connected with the socio-economic development and welfare of Safai Karamcharis, by the Central Government:

Provided that at least one of the Members shall be a woman.

4. Terms of Office and Conditions of Service of Chairperson, Vice-Chairperson and Members

(1) The Chairperson, Vice-Chairperson and every Member shall hold office for such period not exceeding three years as may be specified by the Central Government in this behalf or up to the 31st day of March, 1997, whichever is earlier.

(2) The Chairperson, Vice-Chairperson and Member may, by writing under his hand addressed to the Central Government, resign from the office of Chairperson, Vice-Chairperson or, as the case may be, of the Member at any time.

(3) The Central Government shall remove a person from the office of Chairperson, Vice-Chairperson or a Member if that person–

(a) becomes an undischarged insolvent;

(b) is convicted and sentenced to imprisonment for an offence which, in the opinion of the Central Government, involves moral turpitude;

(c) becomes of unsound mind and stands so declared by a competent court;

(d) refuses to act or becomes incapable of acting;

(e) is, without obtaining leave of absence from the Commission, absent from three consecutive meetings of the Commission;

(f) has, in the opinion of the Central Government, so abused the position of Chairperson or Member as to render that person's continuance in office detrimental to the public interest:

Provided that no person shall be removed under this clause until that person has been given reasonable opportunity of being heard in the matter.

(4) A vacancy caused under sub-section (2) or sub-section (3) or otherwise shall be filled by fresh nomination and a person so nominated shall hold office for the unexpired period of the term for which his predecessor in office would have held office if such vacancy had not arisen.

(5) The salaries and allowances payable to, and the other terms and conditions of service of, the Chairperson, Vice-Chairperson and Members shall be such as may be prescribed.

5. Officers and Other Employees of the Commission

(1) The Central Government shall provide the Commission with such officers and employees as may be necessary for the efficient performance of the functions of the Commission under this Act.

(2) The salaries and allowances payable to, and the other terms and conditions of service of, the officers and other employees appointed for the purpose of the Commission shall be such as may be prescribed.

6. Vacancy, etc. not to Invalidate the Proceedings of the Commission

No act or proceeding of the Commission shall be invalid merely on the ground of the existence of any vacancy or defect in the constitution of the Commission.

7. Procedure to be regulated by the Commission

(1) The Commission shall meet as and when necessary and shall meet at such time and place as the Chairperson may think fit.

(2) The Commission shall regulate its own procedure.

(3) All orders and decisions of the Commissions shall be authenticated by the Chairperson or any other office of the Commission duly authorised by the Chairperson in this behalf.

CHAPTER III
FUNCTIONS AND POWERS OF THE COMMISSION

8. Functions and Powers of the Commission

(1) The Commission shall perform all or any of the following functions, namely:

(a) recommend to the Central Government specific programmes of action towards elimination of inequalities in status, facilities and opportunities for Safai Karamcharis under a time-bound action plan;

(b) study and evaluate the implementation of the programmes and schemes relating to the social and economic rehabilitation of Safai Karamcharis and make recommendations to the Central Government and State Government for better co-ordination and implementation of such programmes and schemes;

(c) investigate specific grievances and take *suo moto* notice of matters relating to non-implementation of–

(i) programmes or schemes in respect of any group of Safai Karamcharis;

(ii) decisions, guidelines or instructions, aimed at mitigating the hardship of Safai Karamcharis;

(iii) measures for the social and economic upliftment of Safai Karamcharis;

(iv) the provisions of any law in its application to Safai Karamcharis; and take up such matters with the concerned authorities or with the Central or State Government;

(d) make periodical reports to the Central and State Governments on any matter concerning Safai Karamcharis, taking into account any difficulties or disabilities being encountered by Safai Karamcharis;

(e) any other matter which may be referred to it by the Central Government.

(2) In the discharge of its functions under sub-section (1), the Commission shall have power to call for information with respect to any matter specified in that sub-section from any Government or local or other authority.

CHAPTER IV
MISCELLANEOUS

9. Chairperson, Vice-Chairperson and Members and Staff of the Commission to be Public Servants

The Chairperson, Vice-Chairperson, Members, officers and other employees of the Commission shall be deemed to be public servants within the meaning of section 21 of the Indian Penal Code.

10. Central Government to Consult Commission

The Central Government shall consult the Commission on all major policy matters affecting Safai Karamcharis.

11. Annual Report

The Commission shall prepare, in such form and at such time, for each financial year, as may be prescribed, its annual report, giving a full account of its activities during the previous financial year and forward a copy thereof to the Central Government.

12. Annual Report to be laid before Parliament or the Legislative Assembly

(1) The Central Government shall cause the annual report to be laid before each House of Parliament along with memorandum explaining the action taken or proposed to be taken on the recommendations contained therein in so far as they relate to the Central Government and the reasons for non-acceptance, if any, of any such recommendation.

(2) Where the said report or any part thereof relates to any matter with which a State Government is concerned, a copy of such report shall be forwarded to the Governor of the State who shall cause it to be laid before the Legislature of the State along with a memorandum explaining the action taken or proposed to be taken on the recommendations relating to the State and the reasons for non-acceptance, if any, of any such recommendation or part.

13. Delegation of Powers

The Commission may, be general or special order, delegate to the Chairperson, Vice-Chairperson or any Member or to any officer of the Commission subject to such conditions and limitations, if any, as may be specified therein, such of its powers and duties under this Act as it may deem fit.

14. Protection of Action taken in Good Faith

No suit, prosecution or other legal proceeding shall lie against the Central Government, Commission, Chairperson, Vice-Chairperson, Members or any officer or other employee of the Commission for anything which is in good faith done or intended to be done under this Act.

15. Power to make Rules

(1) The Central Government may, by notification in the Official Gazette, make rules for carrying out the provisions of this Act.

(2) In particular, and without prejudice to the generality of the foregoing powers, such rules may provide for all or any of the following matters, namely:

(a) salaries and allowances payable to, and other terms and conditions of service of, the Chairperson, Vice-Chairperson and Members under sub-section (5) of section 4 and of officers and other employees under sub-section (2) of section 5;

(b) the form in, and the time at, which the annual report shall be prepared under Section 11;

(c) any other matter which is required to be, or may be, prescribed.

(3) Every rule made under this Act shall be laid, as soon as may be after it is made, before each House of Parliament, while it is in session, for a total period of thirty days which may be comprised in one session or in two or more successive sessions, and if, before the expiry of the session immediately following the session or the successive sessions aforesaid, both Houses agree in making any modification in the rule or both Houses agree that the rule should not be made, the rule shall thereafter have effect only in such modified form or be of no effect, as the case may be; so, however, that any such modification or annulment shall be without prejudice to the validity of anything previously done under that rule.

The Employment of Manual Scavengers and Construction of Dry Latrines (Prohibition) Act, 1993

No. 46 of 1993

[5th June, 1993]

An Act to provide for the prohibition of employment of manual scavengers as well as construction or continuance of dry latrines and for the regulation of construction and maintenance of water-seal latrines and for matters connected therewith or incidental thereto.

WHEREAS fraternity assuring the dignity of the individual has been enshrined in the Preamble to the Constitution;

AND WHEREAS Article 47 of the Constitution, *inter alia*, provided that State shall regard raising the standard of living of its people and the improvement of public health as among its primary duties;

AND WHEREAS the dehumanising practice of manual scavenging of human excreta still continues in many parts of the country;

AND WHEREAS the municipal laws by themselves as a measure for conservation of dry latrines into water-seal latrines and prevention of construction of dry latrines are not stringent enough to eliminate this practice.

AND WHEREAS it is necessary to enact a uniform legislation for the whole of India for abolishing manual scavenging by declaring employment of manual scavengers for removal of human excreta an offence and thereby ban the further proliferation of dry latrines in the country;

AND WHEREAS it is desirable for eliminating the dehumanising practice of employment of manual scavengers and for protecting and improving the human environment to make it obligatory to convert dry latrines into water-seal latrines or to construct water-seal latrines in new constructions;

AND WHEREAS Parliament has no power to make laws for the States with respect to the matters aforesaid, except as provided in articles 249 and 250 of the Constitution;

AND WHEREAS in persuance of Clause (1) of Article 252 of the Constitution, resolutions have been passed by all the Houses of the Legislatures of the States of Andhra Pradesh, Goa, Karnataka, Maharashtra, Tripura and West Bengal that the matters aforesaid should be regulated in those States by Parliament by law;

BE it enacted by Parliament in the Forty-fourth Year of the Republic of India as follows:–

CHAPTER I
PRELIMINARY

1. Short Title, Application and Commencement

(1) This Act may be called the Employment of Manual Scavengers and Construction of Dry Latrines (Prohibition) Act, 1993.

(2) It applies in the first instance to the whole of the States of Andhra Pradesh, Goa, Karnataka, Maharashtra, Tripura and West Bengal and in the Union territories and it shall also apply to such other State which adopts this Act by resolution passed in that behalf under Clause (1) of Article 252 of the Constitution.

(3) It shall come into force in the States of Andhra Pradesh, Goa, Karnataka, Maharashtra, Tripura and West Bengal and in the Union Territories on such date as the Central Government may, by notification, appoint and in any other State which adopts this Act under clause (1) of article 252 of the Constitution, on the date of such adoption.

2. Definitions

In this Act, unless the context otherwise requires,–

(a) "area", in relation to any provision of this Act, means such area as the State Government may, having regard to the requirements of that provision, specify by notification;

(b) "building" means a house, out-house, stable, latrine, urinal, sheet house, hut, wall (other than a boundary wall) or any other structure whether made of masonry, bricks, wood, mud, metal, or other material;

(c) "dry latrine" means a latrine other than a water-seal latrine;

(d) "environment" includes water, air and land and the interrelationship which exists among and between water, air and land and human beings, other living creatures, plants, micro-organism and property;

(e) "environmental pollutant" means any solid, liquid or gaseous substance present in such concentration as may be, or tend to be, injurious to environment;

(f) "environmental pollution" means the presence in the environment of any environmental pollutant;

(g) "Executive Authority" means an Executive Authority appointed under sub-section (1) of section 5;

(h) "HUDCO" means the Housing and Urban Development Corporation Limited, a Government company registered by that name under the Companies Act, 1956 (1 of 1956);

(i) "latrine" means a place set apart for defecation together with the structure comprising such place, the receptacle therein for collection of human excreta and the fittings and apparatus, if any, connected therewith;

(j) "manual scavenger" means a person engaged in or employed for manually carrying human excreta and the expression "manual scavenging" shall be construed accordingly;

(k) "notification" means a notification published in the Official Gazette;

(l) "prescribed" means prescribed by rules under this Act;

(m) "State Government", in relation to a Union territory, means the

Administrator thereof appointed under Article 239 of the Constitution;

(n) "water-seal latrine" means a pour-flush latrine, water flush latrine or a sanitary latrine with a minimum water-seal of 20 millimetres diameter in which excreta is pushed in or flushed by water.

CHAPTER II
PROHIBITION OF EMPLOYMENT OF MANUAL SCAVENGERS, ETC.

3. Prohibition of Employment of Manual Scavengers, etc.

(1) Subject to sub-section (2) and the other provisions of this Act, with effect from such date and in such area as the State Government may, by notification, specify in this behalf, no person shall–

(a) engage in or employ for or permit to be engaged in or employed for any other person for manually carrying human excreta; or

(b) construct or maintain a dry latrine.

(2) The State Government shall not issue a notification under sub-section (1) unless–

(i) it has, by notification, given not less than ninety days' notice of its intention to do so;

(ii) adequate facilities for the use of water-seal latrines in that area exist; and

(iii) it is necessary or expedient to do so for the protection and improvement of the environment or public health in that area.

4. Power to Exempt

The State Government may, by a general or special order published in the Official Gazette, and upon conditions, if any, as it may think fit to impose, exempt any area, category of buildings or class of persons from any provisions of this Act or from any specified requirement contained in this Act or any rule, order, notification or scheme made thereunder or dispense with the observance of any such requirement in a class or classes of cases, if it is satisfied that compliance with such provisions of such requirement is or ought to be exempted or dispensed with in the circumstances of the case.

CHAPTER III
IMPLEMENTING AUTHORITIES AND SCHEMES

5. Appointment of Executive Authorities and their Power and Functions

(1) The State Government may, by order published in the Official Gazette, appoint a District Magistrate or Sub-Divisional Magistrate, as an Executive Authority to exercise jurisdiction within such area as may be specified in the order and confer such powers and impose such duties on him, as may be necessary to ensure that the provisions of this Act are properly carried out and the Executive Authority may specify the officer or officers, subordinate to him, who shall exercise all or any of the powers, and perform all or any of the duties, so conferred or imposed and the local limits within which such powers or duties shall be carried out by the officer or officers so specified.

(2) The Executive Authority appointed under sub-section (1) and the officer or officers specified under that sub-section shall, as far as practicable, try to rehabilitate and promote the welfare of the persons who were engaged in or employed for as manual scavengers in any area in respect of which a notification under sub-section (1) of section 3 has been issued by securing and protecting their economic interests.

6. Power of State Government to make Schemes

(1) The State Government may, by notification, make one or more schemes for regulating conversion of dry latrines into, or construction and maintenance of, water-seal latrines, rehabilitation of the persons who were engaged in or

employed for as manual scavengers in any area in respect of which a notification under sub-section (1) of section 3 has been issued in gainful employment and administration of such schemes and different schemes may be made in relation to different areas and for different purposes of this Act:

Provided that no such scheme as involving financial assistance from the HUDCO shall be made without consulting it.

(2) In particular, and without prejudice to the generality of the foregoing power, such schemes may provide for all or any of the following matters, namely:

(a) time-bound phased programme for the conversion of dry latrines into water-seal latrines;
(b) provision of technical or financial assistance for new or alternate low cost sanitation to local bodies or other agencies;
(c) construction and maintenance of community latrines and regulation of their use on pay and use basis;
(d) construction and maintenance of shared latrines in slum areas or for the benefit of socially and economically backward classes of citizens;
(e) registration of manual scavengers and their rehabilitation;
(f) specification and standards of water-seal latrines;
(g) procedure for conversion of dry latrines into water-seal latrines; and
(h) licensing for collection of fees in respect of community latrines or shared latrines.

7. Power of State Government to issue Directions

Notwithstanding anything contained in any other law but subject to the other provisions of this Act, the State Government may, in the exercise of its powers and performance of its functions under this Act, issue directions in writing to any person, officer or local or other authority and such person, officer or local or other authority shall be bound to comply with such directions.

8. Executive Authorities, Inspectors, Officers and other Employees of such Authorities to be Public Servants

All Executive Authorities, all officers and other employees of such authorities including the officers authorised under sub-section (1) of section 5, all inspectors appointed under sub-section (1) of section 9 and all officers and other employees authorised to execute a scheme or order made under this Act, when acting or purporting to act in pursuance of any provisions of this Act or the rules or schemes made or orders or directions issued thereunder shall be deemed to be public servants within the meaning of section 21 (45 of 1860) of the Indian Penal Code.

9. Appointment of Inspectors and their Powers of Entry and Inspection

(1) The State Government may, by notification, appoint such persons as it may think fit to be inspectors for the purposes of this Act, and define the local limits within which they shall exercise their powers under this Act.

(2) Every inspector within the local limits of jurisdiction of an Executive Authority shall be subordinate to such authority.

(3) Subject to any rules made in this behalf by the State Government, an inspector may, within the local limits of his jurisdiction, enter, at all reasonable times, with such assistance as he considers necessary, any place for the purpose of–

(a) performing any of the functions of the Executive Authority entrusted to him;

(b) determining whether and if so in what manner, any such functions are to be performed or whether any provisions of this Act or the rules, orders or schemes made thereunder or any notice, order, direction or authorisation served, made, given or granted under this Act is being or has been complied with;

(c) examining and testing any latrine or for conducting an inspection of any building in which he has reason to believe that an offence under this Act or the rules, orders or schemes made thereunder has been or is being or is about to be committed and to prevent or mitigate environmental pollution.

10. Power of Executive Authority to Prevent Environmental Pollution in Certain Cases

(1) On receipt of information with respect to the fact or apprehension of any occurrence or contravention of the provisions of Section 3, whether through intimation by some person or on a report of the inspector or otherwise, the Executive Authority shall, early as practicable besides taking any other action under this Act, direct the owner or occupier of the premises to take such remedial measures, as may be necessary, within such reasonable time as may be specified therein and in case the owner or occupier, as the case may be, fails to comply with such directions, cause such remedial measures to be taken as are necessary to prevent or mitigate the environmental pollution at the cost of such owner or occupier of the premises.

(2) The expenses, if any, incurred by the Executive Authority with respect to the remedial measure referred to in sub-section (1), together with interest at such rate as the State Government may specify from the date when a demand for the expenses is made until it is paid, may be recovered by such authority or agency from the person concerned as arrears of land revenue or of public demand.

11. Duty of HUDCO to extend Financial Assistance in Certain Cases

(1) Notwithstanding anything contained in its Memorandum of Association or Articles of Association or schemes for the grant of loans for housing and urban development, it shall be the duty of HUDCO to extend, in suitable cases, financial assistance for the implementation of such schemes for the construction of water-seal latrines as may be made under Section 6.

(2) The financial assistance referred to in sub-section (1) may be extended by HUDCO on such terms and conditions (including on easy and concessional rates of interest) and in such manner as it may think fit in each case or class of cases.

12. Power to Levy Fee

Any order or scheme which the State Government is empowered to make under this Act may notwithstanding the absence of any express provision to that effect provide for levy of fees in respect of–

(a) community latrines constructed under a scheme on pay and use basis; or

(b) shared latrines constructed under a scheme; or

(c) supply of copies of documents or orders of extracts thereof; or

(d) licensing of contractors for construction of water-seal latrines; or

(e) any other purpose or matter involving rendering of service by any officer, committee or authority under this Act or any rule, direction, order or scheme made thereunder:

Provided that the State Government may, if it considers necessary so to do, in the public interest, by general or special order published in the Official Gazette, grant exemption on such grounds as it deems fit from the payment of any such fee either in part or in full.

13. Constitution of the Committees

(1) The Central Government may, by notification, constitute–

(a) one or more Project Committees for appraising of the schemes for the construction of water-seal latrines in the country;

(b) one or more Monitoring Committees to monitor the progress of such schemes; and

(c) such other committees for such purposes of the Act and with such names as the Central Government may deem fit.

(2) The composition of the committees constituted by the Central Government, the powers and functions thereof, the terms and conditions of appointment of the members of such committees and other matters connected therewith shall be such as the Central Government may prescribe.

(3) The members of the committees under sub-section (1) shall be paid such fees and allowances for attending the meetings as may be prescribed.

(4) The State Government may, by notification, constitute–

(a) one or more State Co-ordination Committees for co-ordinating and monitoring of the programmes for the construction of water-seal latrines in the State and rehabilitation of the persons who were engaged in or employed for as manual scavengers in any area in respect of which a notification under sub-section (1) of section 3 has been issued; and

(b) such other committees for such purpose of the Act and with such names as the State Government may deem fit.

(5) The composition of the committees constituted by the State Government the powers and functions thereof, the terms and conditions of the members of such committees and other

matters connected therewith shall be such as the State Government may prescribe.

(6) The members of the committees under sub-section (4) shall be paid such fees and allowances for attending the meetings as may be prescribed.

CHAPTER IV
PENALTIES AND PROCEDURE

14. Penalty for Contravention of the Provisions of the Act and Rules, Orders, Directions and Schemes

Whoever fails to comply with or contravenes any of the provisions of this Act, or the rules or schemes made or orders or directions issued thereunder, shall, in respect of each such failure or contravention be punishable with imprisonment for a term which may extend to one year or with fine, which may extend to two thousand rupees, or both, and in case the failure or contravention continues, with additional fine which may extend to one hundred rupees for every day during which such failure or contravention continues after the conviction for the first such failure or contravention.

15. Offences by Companies

(1) If the person committing an offence under this Act is a company, the company as well as every person in charge of, and responsible to, the company for the conduct of its business at the time of the commission of the offence, shall be deemed to be guilty of the offence and shall be liable to be proceeded against and punished accordingly:

Provided that nothing contained in this sub-section shall render any such person liable to any punishment, if he proves that the offence was committed without his knowledge or that he exercised all due diligence to prevent the commission of such offence.

(2) Notwithstanding anything contained in subsection (1), where an offence under this Act has been committed by a company and it is proved that the offence has been committed with the consent of connivance of, or that the commission of the offence is attributable to any neglect on the part of any director, manager, managing agent or such other officer of the company, such as director, manager, managing agent or other officer shall also be deemed to be guilty of that offence and shall be liable to be proceeded against and punished accordingly.

Explanation- For the purposes of this section.–

(a) "company" means any body corporate and includes a firm or other association of individuals; and

(b) "director" in relation to a firm means a partner in the firm.

16. Offences to be Cognizable

Notwithstanding anything contained in the Code of Criminal Procedure, 1973 (2 of 1974), every offence under this Act shall be cognizable.

17. Provision in relation to Jurisdiction

(1) No court inferior to that of a Metropolitan Magistrate or a Judicial Magistrate of the first class shall try any offence under this Act.

(2) No prosecution for any offence under this Act shall be instituted except by or with the previous sanction of the Executive Authority.

(3) No court shall take congnizance of any offence under this Act except upon a complaint made by a person generally or specially authorised in this behalf by the Executive Authority.

18. Limitation of Prosecution

No court shall take cognizance of an offence punishable under this Act unless the complaint thereof is made within three months from the date on which the alleged commission of the offence came to the knowledge of the complainant.

CHAPTER V
MISCELLANEOUS

19. Information, Reports or Returns

The Central Government may, in relation to its functions under this Act, from time to time, require any person, officer, State Government or other authority to furnish to it, any prescribed authority or officer any reports, returns, statistics, accounts and other information as may be deemed necessary and such person, officer. State Government or other authority, as the case may be, shall be bound to do so.

20. Protection of Action taken in Good Faith

No suit, prosecution or other legal proceedings shall lie against the Government or any officer or other employee of the Government or any authority constituted under this Act or executing any scheme made under this Act or any member, officer or other employee of such authority or authorities in respect of anything which is done or intended to be done in good faith in pursuance of this Act or the rules or schemes made, or the orders or directions issued, thereunder.

21. Effect of Other Laws and Agreements inconsistent with the Act

(1) Subject to the provisions of sub-section (2), the provisions of this Act, the rules, schemes or orders made thereunder shall have effect notwithstanding anything inconsistent therewith contained in any enactment other than this Act, custom, tradition, contract, agreement or other instrument.

(2) If any act or omission constitutes an offence punishable under this Act and also under any other Act, then, the offender found guilty of such offence shall be liable to be punished under the other Act and not under this Act.

22. Power of Central Government to make Rules

(1) The Central Government may, by notification, make rules to carry out the provisions of this Act.

(2) Without prejudice to the generality of the foregoing power, such rules may provide for all or any of the following matters, namely:

(i) the composition of the Project Committees, Monitoring Committees and other committees constituted by the Central Government under sub-section (1) of section 13, the powers and functions thereof, the number of members and their terms and conditions of appointment and other matters connected therewith; and

(ii) the fees and allowances to be paid to the members of the committees constituted under sub-section (1) of section 13.

(3) Every rule made under this Act shall be laid, as soon as may be after it is made, before each House of Parliament, while it is in session, for a total period of thirty days which may be comprised in one session or in two or more successive sessions, and if, before the expiry of the session immediately following the session or the successive sessions aforesaid, both Houses agree in making any modification in the rule or both Houses agree that the rule should not be made, the rule shall thereafter have effect only in such modified form or be of no effect, as the case may be; so, however, that any such modification of annulment shall be without prejudice to the validity of anything previously done under that rule.

23. Power of State Government to make Rules

(1) The State Government may, by notification, make rules, not being a matter for which the rules are or required to be made by the Central Government, for carrying out the provisions of this Act.

(2) Without prejudice to the generality of the foregoing power, such rules may provide for all or any of the following matters, namely:

(i) the composition of the State Co-ordination Committees and other committees constituted by the State Government under sub-section (4) of section 13, the powers and functions thereof, the number of members and their terms and conditions of appointment and other matters connected therewith;

(ii) the fees and allowances to be paid to the members of the committees constituted under sub-section (4) of section 13;

(iii) any other matter which is required to be, or may be prescribed.

(3) Every rule and every scheme made by the State Government under this Act shall be laid, as soon as may be after it is made, before the State Legislature.

24. Power to remove difficulties

(1) If any difficulty arises in giving effect to the provisions of this Act, the Central Government may, by order published in the Official Gazette, make such provisions, not inconsistent with the provisions of this Act as appear to it to be necessary or expedient for removing the difficulty:

Provided that no such order shall be made in relation to a State after the expiration of the period of three years from the commencement of this Act in State.

(2) Every order made under this section shall, as soon as may be after it is made, be laid before each House of Parliament.

INDEX